Math and Science Workout for the

ACT®

The Princeton Review®

Math and Science Workout for the
ACT®

The Staff of The Princeton Review

PrincetonReview.com

Random House, Inc. New York

The Princeton Review, Inc.
111 Speen Street
Suite 550
Framingham, MA 01701
Email: editorialsupport@review.com

ISBN: 978-0-375-42808-1
ISSN: 2157-6017

Editor: Liz Rutzel
Production Editor: Meave Shelton
Production Coordinator: Kim Howie

Printed in the United States of America on partially
recycled paper.

10 9 8 7 6 5 4 3 2 1

First Edition

Editorial
Seamus Mullarkey, Editorial Director
Laura Braswell, Senior Editor
Liz Rutzel, Editor
Selena Coppock, Editor
Heather Brady, Editor

Random House Publishing Team
Tom Russell, Publisher
Nicole Benhabib, Publishing Manager
Ellen L. Reed, Production Manager
Alison Stoltzfus, Associate Managing Editor

Acknowledgments

The Princeton Review would like to thank the following individuals for their help on this book:

Brian Becker, Cynthia Cowan, Jonah Firestone, Melissa Hendrix, Rob Hennen, Jay Hilsenbeck, Oliver Pope, Henry Price, Neeraj Singh, Christopher Stobart, and Miell Yi.

Contents

Introduction 1

   Fun Facts About the ACT 2

   Strategies 4

Science Introduction 9

   The ACT Science Test 9

   Fun Facts about the Science Test 10

   Personal Order of Difficulty (POOD) 11

   Pacing 12

   POE 12

   The Basic Approach 13

   Summary 18

   Now Passages 19

   Answers 34

   Explanations 35

   Later Passages 43

   Answers 58

   Explanations 59

Math Introduction 67

   Algebra 69

   Plugging In 71

   Plugging In the Answers 75

   Plugging In Drill 80

   Answers 82

   Explanations 83

   Geometry 87

   The Basic Approach 88

   The Formulas 90

   Plane Geometry 93

   Coordinate Geometry 94

   Trigonometry 97

   Geometry Drills 101

   Answers 108

   Explanations 109

Comprehensive Math Drill.. 115

Answers 134

Explanations.. 135

Introduction

WELCOME

The ACT is an important part of college admissions. While many schools do not require applicants to submit either ACT or SAT scores, most require one of them. For a long time, different schools would accept only one or the other. If you wanted to apply to schools in the Midwest, you took the ACT, but if you wanted to apply to schools on the East or West Coast, you took the SAT.

The good news is that these rules are obsolete. All schools that require a standardized test will take either the ACT or SAT.

This is good news indeed for test-takers. While there are many similarities between the two tests, many students find they do better on one than the other. The expert advice of The Princeton Review is to take whichever test whose practice version you do better on. While you can certainly take both, you should focus your efforts on one for substantive score improvement. True improvement takes hard work, and it can be tough to become an expert in both. And because schools will take either one, you won't win any brownie points for punishing yourself.

Because you bought this book, we assume you've already made the decision to boost your ACT score. This book provides a strategic and efficient way to improve your scores specifically on Math and Science. For a more thorough review of content and exhaustive practice, we recommend *Cracking the ACT 2011* and *1,296 ACT Practice Questions*.

For more on admissions, see The Princeton Review's *The Best 373 Colleges* or visit our website, PrincetonReview.com

See The Princeton Review's companion book, *English and Reading Workout for the ACT*

FUN FACTS ABOUT THE ACT

The ACT is nothing like the math and science tests you take in school. All of the content review and strategies we teach in the following lessons are based on the specific structure and format of the ACT. Before you can beat a test, you have to know how it's built.

Structure

The ACT is made up of 4 multiple-choice tests and an optional Writing test.

The 5 tests are always given in the same order.

English	Math	Reading	Science	Writing
45 minutes	60 minutes	35 minutes	35 minutes	30 minutes
75 questions	60 questions	40 questions	40 questions	1 Essay

Scoring

When students and schools talk about ACT scores, they mean the composite score, a range of 1–36. The composite is an average of the 4 multiple-choice tests, each scored on the same 1–36 scale. Neither the Writing test score nor the combined English plus Writing score affects the composite.

It's All About the Composite

Whether you look at your score online or wait to get it in the mail, the biggest number on the page is always the composite. While admissions offices will certainly see the individual scores of all 5 tests (and their subscores), schools will use the composite to evaluate your application, and that's why in the end it's the only one that matters.

The composite is an average: Let the full weight of that sink in. Do you need to bring up all 4 scores equally to raise your composite? Do you need to be a superstar in all 4 tests? Should you focus more on your weaknesses than your strengths? No, no, and absolutely not. The best way to improve your composite is to shore up your weaknesses but exploit your strengths as much as possible.

> To improve your ACT score, use your strengths to lift the composite score as high as possible.

You don't need to be a rock star on all 4 tests. Identify 2, maybe 3 tests, and focus on raising those scores as much as you can to raise your composite. Work on your weakest scores to keep them from pulling you down. Think of it this way: If you had only one hour to devote to practice the week before the ACT, put that hour to your best subjects.

Math and Science Scores

These two subjects make a good pair. Every student is different, but many students begin with Math as one of their higher scores and Science as one of the lower. There are good reasons for this. The Math test, perhaps deceptively so, resembles school tests more than the other three. Science feels the most different, and many students are intimidated by both the content and format.

When it comes to improving scores, many students find Math scores the easiest to bring up. A strategic review of the rules and formulas coupled with rigorous practice can add several points. Science, on the other hand, can be the most difficult. The Science test is designed to test your reasoning skills using passage-based information, not tap specific outside knowledge. There are no rules or content you can review. Who knows what specific topics will appear on the next ACT? On the goods-news front, however, The Princeton Review can teach you a smart, effective approach designed to maximize your performance every time, regardless of content. It can be tough to change your ways, but dedicated practice with a strategic method can prevent the Science score from pulling down that composite.

Time

How often do you take a final exam in school that gives you *at most* a minute per question? Probably never. The ACT isn't a school test, and you can't approach it as if it is. While speed and accuracy depend on individual skills and grasp of content, almost all students struggle to finish the Math and Science tests on time. The more you treat these tests the same way you would a school final, the less likely you are to finish, much less finish with the greatest accuracy. The Princeton Review's strategies are all based on this time crunch: There's a difference between knowing *how* to do a question under the best of circumstance and getting it *right* with a ticking clock and glowering proctor in the room.

STRATEGIES

You will raise your ACT score by working smarter, not harder, and a smart test-taker is a strategic test-taker. You will target specific content to review, you will apply an effective and efficient approach, and you will employ the common sense that frequently deserts many of us when we pick up a number 2 pencil.

Each test on the ACT demands a different approach, and even the most universal strategies vary in their applications. In the chapters that follow, we'll discuss these terms in greater detail customized to Math and Science.

Personal Order of Difficulty (POOD)

If time is going to run out, would you rather it run out on the most difficult questions or on the easiest questions? Of course you want it to run out on the points you are less likely to get right. The trick is to find all of the easiest questions and get them done first.

Now

Does a question look okay? Do you know how to do it? Do it *Now*.

Later

Does a question make you go, "hmm"? If you can't find a way to get your pencil moving right away, consider leaving it and coming back *Later*. Circle the question number for easy reference to return.

The Best Way to Bubble In

Work a page at a time, circling your answers right on the booklet. Transfer a page's worth of answers to the Scantron at one time. It's better to stay focused on working questions rather than disrupt your concentration to find where you left off on the Scantron. You'll be more accurate at both tasks. Do not wait to the end, however, to transfer all the answers of that test on your Scantron. Go a page at a time.

Never

Test-taker, know thyself. Know the topics that are your worst and learn the signs that flash danger. Don't waste time on questions you should *Never* do. Instead, use more time to answer the Now and Later questions accurately.

Letter of the Day (LOTD)   Just because you don't *work* a questions doesn't mean you don't *answer* it. There is no penalty for wrong answers on the ACT, so you should never leave any blanks on your Scantron. When you guess on Never questions, pick your favorite two-letter combo of answers and stick with it. For example, always choose A/F or C/H. If you're consistent, you're statistically more likely to pick up more points.

Process of Elimination (POE)

In a perfect world, you'll know how to work all of your Now and Later questions, quickly and accurately, circling the correct answer among the choices. The ACT is *not* a perfect world. But even with a ticking clock and a number 2 pencil in your sweaty hand, wrong answers can be obvious. POE can be a great Plan B on Math when you're stuck, or it may be the best way to find the correct answer on Science. But even when you can't narrow the answers to only one, using POE to get rid of at least one or two wrong answers will substantially increase your odds of getting a question right.

Pacing

The ACT may be designed for you to run out of time, but you can't rush through it as quickly as possible. All you'll do is make careless errors on easy questions you should get right and spend way too much time on difficult ones you're unlikely to get right.

To hit your target score, you have to know how many raw points you need. Use the entire time allotted where it will do the most good: Go slowly enough to avoid careless errors on Now questions, but quickly enough to get to as many Later questions as you need to hit your goal.

On each test of the ACT, the number of correct answers converts to a scaled score of 1–36. ACT works hard to adjust the scale of each test at each administration as necessary to make all scaled scores comparable, smoothing out any differences in level of difficulty across test dates. Thus, there is no truth to any one test date being "easier" than the others, but you can expect to see slight variation in the scale from test to test.

This is the scale from the free test ACT makes available on its website, act.org. We're going to use it to explain how to pick a target score and pace yourself.

Math Pacing

Scale Score	Raw Score	Scale Score	Raw Score	Scale Score	Raw Score
36	60	27	45–47	18	24–25
35	59	26	42–44	17	21–23
34	58	25	40–41	16	17–20
33	56–57	24	37–39	15	14–16
32	55	23	35–36	14	11–13
31	54	22	33–34	13	9–10
30	52–53	21	31–32	12	7–8
29	50–51	20	29–30	11	6
28	48–49	19	26–28	10	5

Our advice is to add 5 questions to your targeted raw score. You have a cushion to get a few wrong—nobody's perfect—and you're likely to pick up at least a few points from your LOTDs. Track your progress on practice tests to pinpoint your target score.

Let's say your goal on Math is a 24. Find 24 under the scaled score column, and you'll see that you need 37–39 raw points. Take all 60 minutes and work 45 questions, using your Letter of the Day on 15 Never questions. With 60 minutes to work on just 45 questions, you'll raise your accuracy on the Now and Later questions. You may get a few wrong, but you're also likely to pick up a few points in your LOTDs, and you should hit your target score of 24. Spend more time to do fewer questions, and you'll raise your accuracy.

Here's another way to think about pacing. Let's say your goal is to move from a 24 to a 27. How many more raw points do you need? As few as 6. Do you think you could find 6 careless errors on your last practice test that you *should* have gotten right?

Science Pacing

Scale Score	Raw Score	Scale Score	Raw Score	Scale Score	Raw Score
36	40	27	32	18	16–17
35	39	26	30–31	17	15
34	--	25	28–29	16	14
33	38	24	26–27	15	13
32	37	23	25	14	12
31	--	22	23–24	13	11
30	36	21	21–22	12	10
29	35	20	19–20	11	9
28	33–34	19	18	10	7–8

For Science pacing is less scientific, no pun intended, than it is for Math. In the lesson that follows, we'll teach you how to pick the best passages to do first. But even the easiest passages will have some tough questions.

Our advice is to be aggressive. Spend the time needed on the easiest passages first, but keep moving to get to your targeted raw score. Use this chart below to figure out how many passages to work.

Target Score	# of Passages to Attempt
< 20	5 passages
20–23	5–6 passages
24–27	6–7 passages
> 27	7 passages

Be Ruthless

The worst mistake a test-taker can make is to throw good time after bad. You read a question and don't understand it, so you read it again. And again. If you stare at it really hard, you know you're going to just *see* it. And you can't move on, because really, after spending all that time it would be a waste not to keep at it, right? Actually, that way of thinking couldn't be more wrong.

You can't let one tough question drag you down. Instead, the best way to improve your ACT score is to follow our advice.

1. Use the techniques and strategies in the lessons to work efficiently and accurately through all your Now and Later questions.
2. Know your Never questions, and use your LOTD.
3. Know when to move on. Use POE, and guess from what's left.

Now move on to the lessons and learn the best way to approach the content.

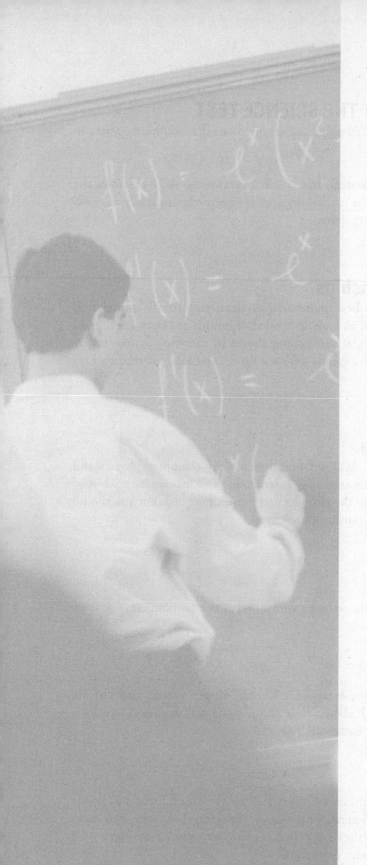

Science
Introduction

THE ACT SCIENCE TEST

For many students, the Science test is the most difficult. Whether the subject matter alone intimidates or the time crunch stresses, the Science test can be difficult to finish. In this chapter, you'll learn how to order the passages and apply a basic approach that makes the most of the time you have.

FUN FACTS ABOUT THE SCIENCE TEST

The Science test consists of 7 passages and 40 questions that you must answer in 35 minutes.

This is not a test of science content, but of science reasoning. ACT describes the necessary skills required for the natural sciences as "interpretation, analysis, evaluation, reasoning, and problem solving."

Trends and Relationships

We think all those skills are best understood as identifying trends and relationships. Whether you are asked to look up a value or synthesize information, it all comes down to the patterns and connections shown by variables, figures, experiments, and scientists. Look for trends *within* a figure, and look for relationships *between* figures.

Outside Knowledge

For the topics of the passages, ACT will pull from biology, chemistry, physics, and the Earth/space sciences, such as geology, astronomy, and meteorology. Most of the questions are answered by the passages and figures provided, but you should also expect 2–3 questions on outside knowledge.

The Passages

On each ACT, the order of the passages will vary, but the distribution of passage types is always the same.

Charts and Graphs

ACT calls these "Data Representations." We call them "Charts and Graphs" because that's what they're all about. They *always* come with figures. There are 3 Charts and Graphs passages, each with 5 questions.

Experiments

ACT calls these "Research Summaries." They look a lot like the Charts and Graphs passages because they *usually* come with figures. However, they come with more reading because they include the descriptions of the experiment set up. There are 3 Experiments passages, each with 6 questions.

Fighting Scientists

ACT calls these "Conflicting Viewpoints," but admit it: Our name is way more fun. There is only one Fighting Scientists passage, featuring 7 questions, on each ACT. It is inherently different from the other 6, even if it *sometimes* comes with figures. The fundamental task of the Fighting Scientists passage is to compare and contrast opposing views of an issue.

PERSONAL ORDER OF DIFFICULTY (POOD)

There are many factors about the structure of this test that make it difficult. It's last, which doesn't help at all. But even if it were first, many would find it the most challenging. Science phobes are intimidated by the subject matter. Science geeks are thwarted by the time crunch. Pick your poison; no one benefits from following ACT's order. On every ACT, you need to work the passages in an order that makes sense for you.

Now Passages

Every time you take the ACT, for practice and for real, pick the order of the passages that makes sense for you. The best passages to do Now are those with the most transparent relationships. When you pick your Now passages, choose exclusively among the Charts and Graphs and Experiments passages. By nature the Fighting Scientists passage is different, and even superior readers find it takes longer to work than the best of the Now passages. So what makes a good Now passage? There are five signs to abide by.

1. Small Tables and Graphs

A good Now passage can have only tables, only graphs, or both. Tables should be no more than 3–4 rows or columns, and graphs should have no more than 3–4 curves.

2. Easy-to-Spot Consistent Trends

Look for graphs with all the curves heading in the same direction: all up, all down, or all flat. Look for tables with numbers in a consistent direction: up, down, or flat.

3. Numbers, not Words or Symbols

To show a consistent trend, the figure has to feature numbers, not words or symbols.

4. Short Answers

Look for as many questions as possible with short answers, specifically answers with values and short relationship words like "increase" or "decrease."

5. Your Science POOD

Don't forget to factor in your familiarity and comfort with the topic when spotting good Now passages. For example, if you've just studied DNA, a passage on DNA will strike you as easier regardless of how the figures look.

Now versus Easy

We are deliberately calling these Now passages rather than Easy passages. Even a passage with great figures will have 1–2 tough questions, but even the toughest questions are easier to crack when you get the central trends and relationships. On passages with incomprehensible figures, even the easiest questions will take you longer because you will keep asking yourself, "What is this saying again?" You'll always work good Now passages more quickly, and good time management is what the ACT is all about.

PACING

With just 35 minutes to do 7 passages and 40 questions, you have an average of 5 minutes for every passage. But should you spend 5 minutes on every passage? Of course not. If you make smart choices of good Now passages, you should be able to work them in less time, leaving yourself more time on the tougher passages. Think about the pacing chart we discussed in Chapter 1. Think about how many points you need to hit your goal.

Be Ruthless and Flexible

Need More Practice?
1,296 ACT Practice Questions provides 6 tests' worth of Science passages. That's 42 passages and 240 questions.

Every Now passage will have 1–2 tough questions, just as every Later passage will have at least 1–2 easy questions. Use Chapters 3 and 4 to practice, but even on the Now passages, know when to guess on a tough question and move onto the next passage. Don't let one tough question drag you down.

POE

The most direct Science questions will ask you to look up a value or a relationship. But the most complex will ask you to synthesize information or draw a conclusion. The more difficult the question, the less it will help to just stare at the figure waiting for divine guidance to help you magically *see* the answer. As is often the case on the ACT, spotting the wrong answers can be much easier than magically divining the right answers. In our 3-step Basic Approach, we'll discuss in greater detail how to use POE.

THE BASIC APPROACH

The most efficient way to boost your Science score is to pick your order and apply our 3-step Basic Approach to passages with figures. Follow our smart, effective strategy to earn as many points as you can.

> **Fighting Scientists**
> The Fighting Scientists passage is fundamentally different from the Charts and Graphs and Experiments passages and requires a different approach. In *Cracking the ACT 2011* we teach you how to approach the Fighting Scientists passage.

Step 1: Work the Figures

Take 10–30 seconds to review your figures. What are the variables? What are the units? In what direction do the variables move?

Graphs present trends visually. For tables, you need to make it visual. Mark the trends for each variable with an arrow. Here are three tables from a good Now passage with the trends marked.

Passage II

Table 1	
Angle between axis of first and second filters (degrees)	Intensity of emerging beam (W/m^2)
0	4.00
15	3.73
30	2.99
45	2.01
60	1.00
75	0.27
90	0.00

↑   ↓

Table 2	
Angle between axis of first and second filters (degrees)	Intensity of emerging beam (W/m^2)
0	8.00
15	7.46
30	6.01
45	3.99
60	2.00
75	0.54
90	0.00

↑   ↓

Table 3	
Angle between axis of first and second filters (degrees)	Intensity of emerging beam (W/m²)
0	6.01
15	5.60
30	4.49
45	2.99
60	1.50
75	0.41
90	0.00

↑   ↓

Step 2: Work the Questions

For each question, look up the value or relationship on the figures as directed. Use your POOD to leave for Later tougher questions. Read if and only when you can't answer a question from the figures.

Try an example.

12. In Experiment 1, if the angle between the axes of polarization increases by 15°, the intensity of the resulting beam:

　　F. halves.
　　G. doubles.
　　H. increases, but not by any constant factor.
　　J. decreases, but not by any constant factor.

Here's How to Crack It

Because you've already marked the trends, you know that as the angle increases, the intensity decreases. Eliminate choices (G) and (H). Look closely at the trend, and choose (J).

Both the Charts and Graphs and Experiments passages will include actual text. Read the passage intros and experiment descriptions *only* when you can't answer a question from a figure.

———————◯———————

Try another example.

———————◯———————

10. How does the setup of Experiment 1 differ from that of Experiment 2 ?

   F. In Experiment 1, the original beam was polarized, but in Experiment 2, it was unpolarized.
   G. In Experiment 1, the original beam was unpolarized, but in Experiment 2, it was polarized.
   H. In Experiment 1, the scientists tested a wider range of angles than they did in Experiment 2.
   J. In Experiment 1, the original beam of light was more intense than the one in Experiment 2.

Here's How to Crack It

The variables are the same in Tables 1 and 2. To answer this question, you have to read the experiment descriptions.

Experiment 1

   The scientists used a laser emitting unpolarized light. The light was directed toward a polarization filter with an axis of polarization pointing straight up, and then through another whose axis of polarization varied. The scientists chose to describe the axis of the second filter by examining the angle between its axis and the axis of the first filter. The intensity of the original beam was 8 W/m^2 (watts per square meter). Their results are shown in Table 1.

Experiment 2

   The scientists repeated the experimental setup of Experiment 1 but used a source of polarized light polarized in the same direction as the axis of the first polarization filter (straight up). The intensity of the original beam was still 8 W/m^2. The results are shown in Table 2.

The light in Experiment 1 was unpolarized, while the light in Experiment 2 was polarized. Choice (G) provides this information correctly.

———————◯———————

Step 3: Work the Answers

In question 12, the central task involved looking up a relationship you've already marked. You used POE to eliminate two answers, but from the beginning you were in command of the question. On question 10, the difference between the two experiments was addressed in the first line of the experiment descriptions. However, if you didn't spot that, good POE would have eliminated choice (F), and you'd have been able to eliminate choices (H) and (J) as well.

On more difficult questions, POE will always be the best bet. You'll be asked to synthesize information from several figures, evaluate a hypothesis, or draw a conclusion, and it will always be easier to eliminate what the figures and passage disprove.

Try another example.

11. The scientists hypothesize that the color of the original beam of light will affect the intensity of the emerging beam. The frequency of a beam of light determines its color. Which of the following would be the best way to test this hypothesis?

   A. Repeating the experiments using more than two polarizing filters
   B. Repeating the experiments on different planets
   C. Repeating the experiments using beams of both high and low frequencies
   D. Repeating the experiments using different intensities for the original beam

Here's How to Crack It

Use POE. Whenever a question asks about how to test something, eliminate answers that have nothing to do with the goal. The question identifies color as an important variable on intensity and identifies frequency as the determinant of color. Eliminate any choice that doesn't address color or frequency. Only choice (C) is left standing.

Repeat

Steps 3 and 4 repeat: Make your way through the rest of the questions. Look up your answers on the figures, and read only when you can't answer a question from the figures. The less the questions involve a value or relationship, the more you should rely on POE to find the answers.

Now move to Chapter 3 to practice the Basic Approach.

Summary

The Science test is not a test of science content but of science reasoning skills.

Pick your order of the passages.

Now passages feature small tables and graphs with easy-to-spot consistent trends made up of numbers, not words or symbols, and feature short answers.

Use the 3-step Basic Approach.

1. Work the Figures. Note the variables and mark the trends.

2. Work the Questions. Look up answers on your figures. Read if and only when you can't answer a question from a figure.

3. Work the Answers. On tougher questions, lean heavily on POE to eliminate wrong answers.

Now Passages

Moth body coloration (see Figure 1) is a *hereditary* trait that can be passed from organisms to their offspring.

white body coloration   black body coloration

Figure 1

Scientists studied the body coloration of 2 subspecies of moths, *Biston betularia f. typica* and *Biston betularia f. carbonaria*. Both species live in City X. Only *B. betularia f. typica* lives in City Y, while only *B. betularia f. carbonaria* lives in City Z. Both subspecies live on trees found in temperate climates, such as birch. Moths with light body coloration are camouflaged from predators while living on light-colored trees, but are not hidden in heavily polluted areas where the tree bark is darkened. Moths with dark body coloration are camouflaged from predators on trees that are darkened by pollution, but not on light-colored trees.

Study 1

Scientists captured 100 *B. betularia f. typica* and 100 *B. betularia f. carbonaria* in City X. They labeled each one, recorded its color, and released it. Then they calculated the percent of birds having each of the body color intensities on a scale of 1 to 10, with 1 being completely black and 10 being completely white. The researchers followed the same methods with 100 *B. betularia f. typica* moths from City Y and 100 *B. betularia f. carbonaria* moths from City Z. The results of this study are shown in Figure 2.

Study 2

After the end of Study 1, the scientists returned to City Y over the course of 10 years, from 1983 to 1992. During each visit, they captured at least 50 *B. betularia f. typica* moths and measured their body color intensities. They then calculated the average *B. betularia f. typica* body color intensity from the 1–10 scale for each of the 10 years. The scientists noted that during the 10-period, 2 years were particularly wet, while 3 years were especially dry (see Figure 3). During wet years, pollutants tend to be washed from the surfaces of tree bark. During dry years, pollutants are more likely to concentrate on tree bark, and the tree bark itself tends to become thicker.

Figure 2

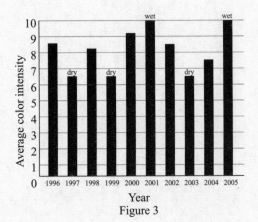

Figure 3

1. Based on the results from Study 1, the largest percentage of moths in City Y and City Z had a color intensity of:

	City Y	City Z
A.	8	1
B.	8	5
C.	9	4
D.	9	5

2. During which of the following years was birch bark most likely to be thickest in City Y?

F. 2000
G. 2001
H. 2002
J. 2003

3. How was Study 1 different from Study 2 ?

A. *B. betularia f. carbonaria* moths were captured in Study 1 but not in Study 2.
B. *B. betularia f. typica* moths were captured in Study 1 but not in Study 2.
C. The moth body coloration was measured in Study 1 but not in Study 2.
D. The moth body coloration was measured in Study 2 but not in Study 1.

4. The scientists most likely labeled the moths in Study 1 to:

F. determine how body coloration was affected by pollution in City X.
G. determine the average wingspan of each population of moths.
H. make sure that the body coloration of each moth was measured only once.
J. make sure that the body coloration of each moth was measured multiple times.

5. Based on the results from Study 2, would a moth with a body color intensity measuring 6.5 or a moth with a body color intensity measuring 9.5 have had a greater chance of surviving in 2005 ?

A. A moth with a body color intensity of 6.5, because pollutants concentrate more on tree bark during dry years.
B. A moth with a body color intensity of 6.5, because pollutants are removed from tree bark during dry years.
C. A moth with a body color intensity of 9.5, because pollutants concentrate more on tree bark during dry years.
D. A moth with a body color intensity of 9.5, because pollutants are removed from tree bark during dry years.

6. A scientist hypothesized that there would be a greater range in body coloration in the *B. betularia f. typica* moths when they are forced to coexist with another subspecies of moths. Do the results from Study 1 support this hypothesis?

F. Yes; the range of body coloration for *B. betularia f. typica* moths was greater in City X than in City Y.
G. Yes; the range of body coloration for *B. betularia f. typica* moths was greater in City Y than in City X.
H. No; the range of body coloration for *B. betularia f. typica* moths was greater in City X than in City Y.
J. No; the range of body coloration for *B. betularia f. typica* moths was greater in City Y than in City X.

Passage II

Ethylene glycol is the main ingredient in antifreeze and has the chemical structure shown below:

Figures 1–3 show how solutions of antifreeze vary as the concentration of ethylene glycol. Concentration is given as the percent ethylene glycol by volume in water (% EG) at atmospheric pressure (101.3 kPa). Figure 1 shows how the melting point (the temperature at which solid antifreeze would begin melting) of antifreeze varies with % EG. Figure 2 shows how the boiling point of antifreeze varies with % EG. Figure 3 shows how the density at 25°C varies with % EG.

Figure 2

Figure 3

Figure 1

7. At 101.3 kPa, which of the following solutions will have the *lowest* freezing point?

   A.   100% EG
   B.   68% EG
   C.   50% EG
   D.   0% EG

8. According to Figure 1, the temperature at which solid anti-freeze begins to melt in a 60% EG solution at 101.3 kPa is closest to which of the following?

   F.   0°C
   G. −12°C
   H. −48°C
   J. −60°C

9. Based on Figure 2, which of the following solutions has a boiling point equal to pure water at 101.3 kPa?

   A.   0% EG
   B.   13% EG
   C.   68% EG
   D. 100% EG

10. At 25°C, as the % EG increases from 0% to 100%, the mass per unit volume:

   F. increases only.
   G. decreases only.
   H. increases, then decreases.
   J. decreases, then increases.

11. According to Figures 2 and 3, a solution of antifreeze that has a density of 1.09 g/mL at 25°C will have a boiling point closest to which of the following?

   A. 100°C
   B. 104°C
   C. 111°C
   D. 122°C

Passage III

A series of studies have been conducted to determine the level of harmful radiation at nuclear-waste clean-up facilities. One method of determining the level of radiation in an area is to measure the growth of certain crystals such as $Bi_4Ge_3O_{12}$ (BGO). BGO crystals come in two basic configurations that grow in environments exposed to high levels of gamma radiation. BGO(I) has a hexagonal crystalline structure and typically grows in environments that are continuously exposed to 100–200 rads of gamma radiation per day, while BGO(II) has an octagonal crystalline structure and typically grows in environments that are continuously exposed to 500–800 rads of gamma radiation per day. Scientists conducted two studies to determine which configuration of BGO crystal would be more useful in determining the amount of exposure to gamma radiation around a nuclear-waste clean-up site.

Study 1

BGO(I) and BGO(II) crystals of 4 cm^3 to 8 cm^3 were collected from a nuclear waste clean-up site west of Phoenix, AZ. Crystals of both types were placed into individually sealed clear-plastic containers. Ten crystals of each type were then exposed to 3 different levels of gamma radiation—150 rads per day, 450 rads per day, and 750 rads per day—for a period of 7 days. The average volume for each type of crystal and each of the 3 levels of radiation was then determined. The results are shown in Figure 1.

Figure 1

Study 2

The BGO (I) and BGO (II) crystals were removed from the radiation sources and weighed. The average mass of the BGO(I) was determined to be about 13 gm. The average mass of the BGO(II) crystals at each of the three levels of radiation is shown in Figure 2.

Figure 2

For each radiation level the volume and mass of the BGO(II) crystals were plotted. The best-fit curve for each is shown in Figure 3.

Figure 3

12. Based on Figure 3, for a radiation level of 450 rads, the size and mass of how many BGO(II) crystals were plotted?

   F. 10
   G. 12
   H. 32
   J. Cannot be determined from the given information

13. Suppose that a fourth group of BGO(II) had been exposed to radiation at a level of 300 rads. After 7 days, the average volume of each of these crystals would have been:

   A. less than 35 cm^3.
   B. between 35 cm^3 and 50 cm^3.
   C. between 50 cm^3 and 60 cm^3.
   D. greater than 60 cm^3.

14. At the end of Study 2, a crystal of BGO(II) was found to have a mass of 10 g and a volume of 100 cm³. Based on Figure 3, this crystal most likely had been exposed to radiations of which of the following levels?

F.   150 rads
G.   300 rads
H.   450 rads
J.   750 rads

15. Which of the following sets of data points most likely yielded the best-fit curve for BGO(II) crystals exposed to 150 rads of radiation?

A.

B.

C.

D.

16. According to the results of Studies 1 and 2, for a given level of radiation, how did the crystals of BGO(I) compare to the crystals of BGO(II)? On average BGO(I) had:

F.   larger volume and greater mass.
G.   larger volume but lesser mass.
H.   smaller volume and lesser mass.
J.   smaller volume but greater mass.

17. Of the 10 crystals of BGO(I) that were exposed to 450 rads of radiation, 2 cracked and 8 remained whole. The total mass of all of the crystals combined can be calculated using which of the following expressions?

A.   13 gm × 10
B.   13 gm + 10
C.   13 gm × 8
D.   13 gm + 8

Passage IV

Leaf area index is a unitless measure of the percent of a rainforest floor that is covered by the leaves of tall trees. Leaf area index may increase because of an increase in *precipitation* (measured as millimeters of rainfall per km^2 per year). Table 1 shows how the leaf area index formed by the *canopy layer* (30 to 45 m above the rainforest floor) varies with precipitation in a 1000 km^2 section of the Amazon Rainforest. Figures 1–3 show the relative precipitation, RP (the percent below the rainfall measured on January 1, 1985), and the monthly average leaf area index of the *emergent layer* (45 to 55 m above the rainforest floor), *canopy layer*, and *understory layer* (0 to 30 m above the rainforest floor), respectively, over from January 1990 to January 2005.

Table 1	
Precipitation (mm/km^2/yr)	Leaf area index
1.80	5.2
1.85	5.4
1.90	5.6
1.95	5.8
2.00	6.0

year
Figure 1

year
Figure 2

year
Figure 3

18. The leaf area index of the canopy layer covering the section of the rainforest in January of the 5th year studied was closest to which of the following?

   F. 4.0
   G. 4.5
   H. 5.0
   J. 5.5

19. Based on Table 1, a precipitation of 1.70 mm/km^2/yr would correspond to a leaf area index that is closest to which of the following?

   A. 4.8
   B. 5.5
   C. 6.0
   D. 6.5

20. A botanist states, "The leaf area index of the understory layer is more directly correlated with annual precipitation than is the leaf area index of the canopy layer." Is this statement consistent with Figures 1 and 3 ?

   F. No, because the plot for the leaf area index of the canopy layer more closely resembles the plot for the annual precipitation.
   G. No, because the plot for the leaf area index of the understory layer more closely resembles the plot for the annual precipitation.
   H. Yes, because the plot for the leaf area index of the canopy layer more closely resembles the plot for the annual precipitation.
   J. Yes, because the plot for the leaf area index of the understory layer more closely resembles the plot for the annual precipitation.

21. Which of the following figures best represents the leaf area index measured in the 7th year of the study?

22. The emergent layer is primarily composed of small leaves that cover a wide area, while the understory layer is primarily composed of broad leaves that cover a small area. This difference is most likely because the average precipitation at heights of:

F. 0 to 30 m above the rainforest floor is above 2.00 mm/km²/yr, whereas the average precipitation at heights of 30–45 m above the rainforest floor is below 1.80 mm/km²/yr.

G. 0 to 30 m above the rainforest floor is above 2.00 mm/km²/yr, whereas the average precipitation at heights of 45–55 m above the rainforest floor is below 1.80 mm/km²/yr.

H. 0 to 30 m above the rainforest floor is below 1.80 mm/km²/yr, whereas the average precipitation at heights of 30–45 m above the rainforest floor is above 2.00 mm/km²/yr.

J. 0 to 30 m above the rainforest floor is below 1.80 mm/km²/yr, whereas the average precipitation at heights of 45–55 m above the rainforest floor is above 2.00 mm/km²/yr.

Passage V

In 1789, Mt. Mantu erupted off the coast of Brunei releasing a cloud of ash that lowered global temperatures for 15 years. When a volcano erupts, it releases a cloud of ash, dust, and debris into the atmosphere thousands of times the volume of the volcano. In addition, at the time of the eruption, the volcano produces a mud and ash flow along the sides of the volcano. The ash flow around Mt. Mantu covered an area 30 times larger than the original size of the volcano. Figure 1 shows the volume of the ash clouds released by volcanoes of differing diameters during the last 200 million years.

Figure 2 shows the average amount of time elapsed between consecutive major eruptions of various volcanoes of similar sizes, for a range of volcano sizes. Figure 3 represents the percentage of land area covered by volcanic ash flows in three different mountain ranges—the Cascades, the Appalachians, and the Himalayas—for various volcanic ash flow diameters.

Figure 1

Figure 2

23. If 100 km³ of ash was released by Mt. Mantu, according to Figure 1, Mt. Mantu's diameter was most likely closest to which of the following?

   A. 0.02 km
   B. 0.01 km
   C. 0.1 km
   D. 1 km

24. According to Figure 2, for progressively larger volcanoes, the average amount of time that elapses between consecutive eruptions with the same diameter:

   F. increases only.
   G. decreases only.
   H. varies, but with no general trend.
   J. remains the same.

25. According to Figure 3, for any given range of volcanic ash flows, the percent of area covered in the Himalayas by ash flows is:

   A. less than the Cascades and the Appalachians.
   B. less than the Cascades but greater than the Appalachians.
   C. greater than the Cascades or than the Appalachians.
   D. greater than the Cascades but less than the Appalachians.

26. Suppose a volcano similar to Mt. Mantu created an ash flow that was 30 km in diameter. Based on Figure 1 and other information provided, that volcano would have released a volume of ash closest to which of the following?

    F.   5,000 km^3

    G.   10,000 km^3

    H.   50,000 km^3

    J.   100,000 km^3

27. Assume that a volcano with a diameter of 30 km erupted 500,000 years ago. Also assume that another volcano 30 km in diameter will erupt in the future. If the time that elapses between eruptions is equal to the average amount of time a given in Figure 2, a 30 km in diameter volcano should erupt approximately:

    A.   250,000 years from now.

    B.   500,000 years from now.

    C. 1,000,000 years from now.

    D. 1,500,000 years from now.

Passage VI

An astrophysics class is given the following facts about the burning out of stars.

1. The burning out of a star can be divided into 3 stages: *helium fusion*, *planetary nebula formation*, and *white dwarf development*.

2. Mid-sized stars fuse hydrogen nuclei (composed of protons) into helium nuclei at their centers, in a process known as helium fusion. These include yellow dwarves, like our Sun, and the slightly smaller orange dwarves. Helium fusion releases a significant amount of kinetic energy.

3. As kinetic energy continues to be released, a planetary nebula may form, in which colorful, ionized gas spreads out from the star's center.

4. The remaining material at the center of the planetary nebula condenses into a white dwarf, which is relatively cool and small in size.

5. Red dwarves are smaller stars that can also carry out helium fusion. These stars can develop into white dwarves sooner than yellow and orange dwarves, and do not form planetary nebulas.

Two students discuss the eventual fate of three stars in the Alpha Centauri system. Alpha Centauri A, a 1.10-solar-mass yellow dwarf star, where one *solar mass* unit is equivalent to the mass of the Sun; Alpha Centauri B, a 0.91-solar-mass orange dwarf star; and Alpha Centauri C, a 0.12-solar-mass red dwarf star. Alpha Centauri A and B comprise a binary star system that revolves around a common center of mass, while Alpha Centauri C revolves around a nearby center of mass.

Student 1

The 3 stars of the Alpha Centauri system all formed at the same time from the same collection of matter. Alpha Centauri C was initially the most massive of the three stars, and Alpha Centauri A and Alpha Centauri B had the same size. The large Alpha Centauri C had more helium fusion than the other two stars, so it quickly became the smallest of the stars. More of its matter flowed to Alpha Centauri A than to Alpha Centauri B, making Alpha Centauri A slightly larger than Alpha Centauri B.

Student 2

Alpha Centauri A and Alpha Centauri B formed at a different time than Alpha Centauri C. Alpha Centauri A and Alpha Centauri B formed at the same time from a common collection of matter, and Alpha Centauri A was initially more massive than Alpha Centauri B. Alpha Centauri C formed later from a different, smaller collection of matter, and never became bigger than a red dwarf. At some point, the small Alpha Centauri C was attracted to the other two stars, resulting in a triple star system.

28. Based on Student 2's discussion, Alpha Centauri C is part of the Alpha Centauri system because of which of the following forces exerted on Alpha Centauri C by the original binary star system?

F. Electromagnetism
G. Gravitation
H. Strong nuclear interaction
J. Weak nuclear interaction

29. Based on Student 1's discussion and Fact 2, while matter flowed between Alpha Centauri C and Alpha Centauri A, Alpha Centauri C released most of its energy by fusing:

A. helium nuclei into hydrogen nuclei at its core.
B. hydrogen nuclei into helium nuclei at its core.
C. helium nuclei into hydrogen nuclei at its periphery.
D. hydrogen nuclei into helium nuclei at its periphery.

30. Suppose that stars that form from the same collection of matter have similar chemical composition, but that stars that form from different collections of matter have different chemical compositions. Student 2 would most likely agree with which of the following statements comparing chemical compositions of the stars in the current Alpha Centauri system at the time that they were formed.

F. Alpha Centauri A and Alpha Centauri B had the most similar compositions.
G. Alpha Centauri A and Alpha Centauri C had the most similar compositions.
H. Alpha Centauri B and Alpha Centauri C had the most similar compositions.
J. Alpha Centauri A, Alpha Centauri B, Alpha Centauri C all had the same compositions.

31. If the mass of the Sun is 2.0×10^{33} g, what is the mass of Alpha Centauri A?

A. 1.8×10^{33} g
B. 2.0×10^{33} g
C. 2.2×10^{33} g
D. 2.4×10^{32} g

32. Which of the following statements best explains why the process described in Fact 2 requires a high initial temperature and pressure?

F. All electrons are negatively charged, and like charges attract each other.
G. All electrons are negatively charged, and like charges repel each other.
H. All protons are positively charged, and like charges attract each other.
J. All protons are positively charged, and like charges repel each other.

33. Based on Fact 5 and Student 1's discussion, which of the 3 stars in the Alpha Centauri system, if any, is most likely to develop into a white dwarf?

   A. Alpha Centauri A
   B. Alpha Centauri B
   C. Alpha Centauri C
   D. The three stars will likely develop into white dwarves at the same time.

34. Based on Fact 5, would Student 2 agree that by the time Alpha Centauri B develops into a white dwarf, it will have spent as much time as a mid-sized star as Alpha Centauri A?

   F. Yes, because according to Student 2, Alpha Centauri A has always been less massive than Alpha Centauri B.
   G. Yes, because according to Student 2, Alpha Centauri A has always been more massive than Alpha Centauri B.
   H. No, because according to Student 2, Alpha Centauri A has always been less massive than Alpha Centauri B.
   J. No, because according to Student 2, Alpha Centauri A has always been more massive than Alpha Centauri B.

Electromagnets are used in a variety of industrial processes and often consist of a large *solenoid*, a helical coil of wire, that produces a uniform *magnetic field strength* B, when current I, passes through it (see Figure 1).

Figure 1

The magnetic field of a solenoid is a factor of its resistance to changes in current, a property called *inductance* (L). The *relative permeability*, μ, is a property of the material within the solenoid coils which may magnify the magnetic field strength.

Figure 2 shows at 25°C, for specific values of μ and l (the length of the solenoid), how B varies with I and with the number of coils (N).

Figure 2

Figure 3 shows, for specific values of A (cross-sectional area of the solenoid) and N, how L varies with l and m at 25°C. In a separate experiment, the *average minimum solenoid length*, l_o, for a solenoid containing 100 coils was determined.

Figure 3

35. For the conditions specified in Figure 2 and I = 0.75 Amps, the solenoid will attract iron metal particles most strongly when the number of coils is closest to which of the following?

A. 0 coils
B. 40 coils
C. 120 coils
D. 200 coils

36. According to Figure 3, does l_o vary with μ ?

F. Yes; as μ increases, l_o decreases.
G. Yes; as μ increases, l_o remains the same.
H. No; as μ increases, l_o increases.
J. No; as μ increases, l_o remains the same.

37. According to Figure 3, for $\mu = 14 \times 10^{-5}$ henry/m, as the length of the solenoid increases, L:

A. increases only.
B. decreases only.
C. varies, but with no consistent trend.
D. remains the same.

38. For a given solenoid length, what is the correct ranking of the values of μ in Figure 3, from the μ associated with the highest L to the μ associated with the lowest L?

  F. 7×10^{-5} henry/m, 14×10^{-5} henry/m, 28×10^{-5} henry/m

  G. 14×10^{-5} henry/m, 28×10^{-5} henry/m, 7×10^{-5} henry/m

  H. 7×10^{-5} henry/m, 28×10^{-5} henry/m, 14×10^{-5} henry/m

  J. 28×10^{-5} henry/m, 14×10^{-5} henry/m, 7×10^{-5} henry/m

39. What is the average minimum solenoid length of a solenoid of for the conditions given in Figure 3 ?

  A. 0 m
  B. 0.1 m
  C. 0.2 m
  D. 0.4 m

ANSWERS

Passage I

1. B
2. J
3. A
4. H
5. D
6. F

Passage II

7. B
8. H
9. A
10. F
11. B

Passage III

12. J
13. B
14. H
15. B
16. H
17. C

Passage IV

18. J
19. A
20. F
21. B
22. J

Passage V

23. C
24. F
25. A
26. H
27. B

Passage VI

28. G
29. B
30. F
31. C
32. J
33. C
34. J

Passage VII

35. D
36. J
37. B
38. J
39. B

EXPLANATIONS

Passage I

1. **B** This question asks about Study 1, so we'll need to look at Figure 2. The color intensity for the moths in City *Y* is shown on the right side of the second graph in black, and the highest percentage of these moths had a color intensity of 8. Eliminate choices (C) and (D). The color intensity for the moths in City *X* is shown on the left side of the third graph in gray, and the highest percentage of these moths had a color intensity of 5. Eliminate choice (A), and the only remaining answer is choice (B).

2. **J** The blurb in Study 2 contains the following information: *During dry years, pollutants are more likely to concentrate on tree bark, and the tree bark itself tends to become thicker.* Therefore, bark is thickest during dry years, and of the years listed on Figure 3, only 2003 is listed as a "dry" year, and therefore is the best answer from the given choices.

3. **A** Study 1 contains the following information: *Scientists captured 100* B. betularia f. typica *and 100* B. betularia f. carbonaria *in City X.* Study 2 contains the following information: *During each visit* [from 1983 to 1992], *they captured at least 50* B. betularia f. typica *moths and measured their body color intensities.* Therefore, it can be assumed that they *did not* catch B. bethularia f. carbonaria in Study 2, making choice (A) the best answer. For color intensity, note the axes of each of the graphs. Color intensity is a variable plotted along the *x*-axis in Figure 2 and along the *y*-axis in Figure 3, meaning that it was measured in both studies.

4. **H** Choices (H) and (J) are direct opposites, which means that one of them is likely to be true. You'll need to use a bit of science common sense here to choose between these two. In Study 1, the scientists are trying to count the number of moths in these various cities; therefore, in order to make this count accurate, they will need to make sure that each moth is only counted once, as in choice (H). Choice (F) is incorrect because *pollution* is measured in Study 2, and choice (G) is incorrect because *wingspan* is not measured in either study.

5. **D** Figure 3 shows that 2005 was a wet year, and the average color intensity was 10. First, it is clear that moths with higher color intensities are more likely to survive in the wet years than the dry years, so the moth with a color intensity of 9.5 is more likely to survive than the moth with a color intensity of 6.5. Eliminate choices (A) and (B). Then, notice that Study 2 contains the following information: *During wet years, pollutants tend to be washed from the surfaces of tree bark.* This information agrees with choice (D).

6. F   This question is difficult to answer "Yes" or "No" immediately, so work with the reasons given in each of the answer choices. In City *X*, the coloration of *B. betularia f. typica* ranges from 5 to 10. In City *Y*, the coloration of *B. betularia f. typica* ranges from only 7 to 10. Eliminate choices (G) and (J). The hypothesis that a greater range in body coloration is produced by a diversity in the subspecies is therefore supported by this information, because City *X* contains two subspecies and City *Y* contains only one. This question is tricky: You don't need to use the *y*-axis at all, because nothing in the question asks about the percent of captured moths. The only variable at play is body coloration.

Passage II

7. B   "Freezing point" does not appear on any of the figures, so you'll need a bit of outside knowledge here. Think about it this way: The freezing point is the point at which a substance turns from a liquid into a solid. The melting point is the point at which a substance turns from a solid into a liquid. Therefore, freezing point and melting point are one and the same. Use Figure 1. According to the passage, all readings are taking at atmospheric pressure 101.3 kPa, so you can disregard that part of the question. The melting point of the solution seems to be lowest around 70% EG. The closest of the answers is choice (B), 68%.

8. H   Use Figure 1. According to the passage, all readings are taking at atmospheric pressure 101.3 kPa, so you can disregard that part of the question. According to Figure 1, at 60% EG, the melting point is roughly −48°C, or choice (H).

9. A   The substance that will behave most like pure water and boil at the same temperature would be pure water itself. Choice (A), 0% EG, would mean a solution of no ethylene glycol and all water. Increasing the % EG, as in choices (B), (C), and (D), and therefore decreasing the percentage of water, would make the solution behave less like water.

10. F   This question requires a bit of outside knowledge: "density" and "mass per unit length" are one in the same. Therefore, you can use Figure 3 to answer this question even though the word "density" does not appear explicitly in this question. According to the passage, all density readings are taken at a temperature of 25°C, so you can disregard that temperature and just look at the graph. According to this graph, as % EG increases, the density steadily increases as well. The best answer, therefore, comes from choice (F).

11. B   According to Figure 2, a substance with a density of 1.09 g/mL has 40% EG. Use this EG value on Figure 3. According to Figure 3, a substance with 40% EG has a boiling point of approximately 104°C. Only choice (B) works.

Passage III

12. J   The axes given in Figure 3 are "Crystal mass (g)" and "Crystal volume (cm³)." According to the key, different levels of radiation were measured. Nowhere in any of these axes or curves do we have any indication of the *number of crystals* measured. Without this information, and without any relevant information in the introduction, we can't determine how many crystals were measured, making choice (J) the only possible answer.

13. B   Although this question does not mention one specific figure, look at the variables to be compared. We'll need to make a prediction about Volume based on Radiation level. The only one of the three figures that compares these two variables is Figure 1. According to the information in Study 1, these readings were taken after *a period of 7 days*, so we can disregard that bit of information from the question. Now, the question asks about BGO(II), which is represented on Figure 1 by the darker of the two bars. According to the figure, as radiation level increases, crystal volume increases. Therefore, it is reasonable to assume that the volume of a crystal with a radiation level of 300 rads will be higher than that of a crystal with a radiation level of 150 rads and lower than that of a crystal with a radiation level of 450 rads. According to Figure 1, a BGO(II) crystal with a radiation level of 150 rads has a volume of 35 cm³, and a BGO(II) crystal with a radiation level of 450 rads has a volume of 50 cm³. Only choice (B) gives the appropriate range of values between these two volumes.

14. H   Plot the information from the problem onto Figure 3. A mass of 10 g and a volume of 100 cm³ match most closely the curve appearing lowest on the figure. According to the key, this is the curve for 450 rads, or choice (H).

15. B   Figure 3 gives the curve for 150 rads, so find the plot in the answer choices that matches up most closely with the curve for 150 rads in Figure 3. Use POE. The curve starts at 0 cm³, heads in an upward direction, and maxes out around 140 cm³. Eliminate choices (A) and (D) because these curves decrease. Eliminate choice (C) because this curve does not start at 0 cm³. Only choice (B) meets all the requirements and is therefore the best answer.

16. H   Use POE. Figure 1 contains a side-by-side comparison of the volumes of the crystals at different radiation levels. The BGO(I) crystals are represented by the lighter bar, and the BGO(II) crystals are represented by the darker bar. In all cases, the BGO(I) crystals had a smaller volume, so eliminate choices (F) and (G). Figure 2 contains the masses of BGO(II), but not BGO(I). According to the passage, though, *The average mass of the BGO(I) was determined to be about 13 gm.* Therefore, since the masses shown in Figure 2 are all well above this value, it can also be inferred that BGO(I)'s mass was smaller, eliminating choice (J).

17. C   According to the passage, *The average mass of the BGO(I) was determined to be about 13 gm.* Therefore, since there are 8 *whole* crystals left at the end of the experiment, their total mass can be found by multiplying the number of seeds by the mass of each: 13 gm × 8, or choice (C).

Passage IV

18. **J**   Make sure you are keeping the curves and axes straight. We're dealing with Figure 2, which shows the data for the *canopy* layer. The question asks about the leaf area index, so we need the solid line and the *y*-axis shown on the left side of the figure. Once all those elements are in place, you find that the leaf-area index in Year 5 was closest to 5.5. Make sure you are dealing with the correct figure and the correct axes given on that figure.

19. **A**   Table 1 shows a direct relationship: As precipitation goes up, leaf-area index goes up. Therefore, we can expect the leaf-area index at 1.70 mm/km²/yr of precipitation to be below the leaf-area index at 1.80 mm/km²/yr. The leaf-area index at 1.80 mm/km²/yr is 5.2, and the only answer choice that gives a value in between is choice (A).

20. **F**   This problem asks about the *canopy* layer and the *understory* layer, so we will need to use Figures 2 and 3. Take a look at these two graphs: The two curves in the *canopy*-layer graph seem to go up and down at roughly the same rate, whereas the two curves in the *understory*-layer graph don't seem to have a consistent relationship. Because the *canopy*-layer graph shows a more consistent relationship, we can eliminate choices (G) and (J). A more consistent *canopy*-layer graph also *disagrees* with the botanist's statement from the problem, eliminating choice (H). Only choice (F) contains the correct answer to the question and the correct reason for that answer.

21. **B**   Use Figures 1, 2, and 3 to determine each of the annual precipitation values in Year 7. This is the dotted curve, and the values are on the *y*-axis on the right side of each figure. For the *emergent* layer shown in Figure 1, the annual precipitation was roughly 1.33. For the *canopy* layer shown in Figure 2, the leaf-area index was roughly 1.0. For the *understory* layer shown in Figure 3, the annual precipitation was roughly 0.67. You don't need to worry about exact figures: *emergent* should be the largest and *understory* should be the smallest. Only choice (B) works.

22. **J**   This question requires a bit of outside knowledge but can be solved with a little bit of common sense. First, sunlight is more likely to hit higher places than lower places, eliminating choices (F) and (G). Then, between choices (H) and (J), we need to choose between the ranges "30 to 45 m above the rainforest floor" in choice (H) and "45 to 55 m above the rainforest floor" in (J). Read the question carefully! It is asking about the *emergent* layer, which according to the introduction is found *45 to 55 m above the rainforest floor*, making choice (J) the only possible answer.

Passage V

23. **C** According to Figure 1, when the volcano releases 100 km³ of ash, its diameter is approximately 0.1 km, or choice (C). If you had trouble with this problem, you may have been looking at the wrong axes.

24. **F** Figure 2 shows a direct relationship. As "Average time elapsed" increases, "Volcano diameter" also increases. Only choice (F) adequately represents this trend.

25. **A** Use POE. Pick any point on the graph: For 1–5% covered, for example, the bar showing the ash-flow of the Himalayas is lower than both the bars for the Cascades and the Appalachians. This same trend holds true for the other percentages as well. Only choice (A) accurately describes this trend.

26. **H** The passage states that Figure 1 *shows the volume of the ash clouds released by of differing diameters*. It also states that the *ash flow around Mt. Mantu covered an area 30 times larger than the original size of the volcano*. Therefore, if the ash flow in the question is 30 km, the original size of the volcano must be 30 times smaller, or 1 km. According to Figure 1, a volcano with a diameter of 1 km will have an ash-cloud volume of approximately 54,000 km³. Choice (H) gives the best approximation of this value.

27. **B** According to Figure 3, a volcano with a diameter of 30 km should have approximately 1,000,000 years between eruptions. Therefore, since this volcano erupted 500,000 years ago, it will not erupt for another 1,000,000 − 500,00 = 500,000 years, or choice (B).

Passage VI

28. **G** This question requires a bit of outside knowledge. Student 2 concludes with the following sentence: *At some point, the small Alpha Centauri C was attracted to the other two stars, resulting in a triple star system*. Gravity is the attraction between two objects with mass, so attracted matches up most closely with choice (G), *gravitation*. If you picked one of the other answer choices, be careful—the correct answer must have textual support!

29. **B** Student 1's hypothesis contains the following sentence: *The large Alpha Centauri C had more helium fusion than the other two stars, so it quickly became the smallest of the stars*. More of its matter flowed to Alpha Centauri A than to Alpha Centauri B. In other words, Alpha Centauri C released most of its matter by helium fusion. According to Fact 2, mid-sized stars fuse hydrogen nuclei (composed of protons) into helium nuclei at their centers, in a process known as helium fusion. It can therefore be inferred that Alpha Centauri C, in undergoing this process of helium fusion, was fusing hydrogen nuclei into helium nuclei at its center. Only choice (B) contains information consistent with Student 1 and Fact 2.

30. **F** Student 2's hypothesis contains the following sentence: *Alpha Centauri A and Alpha Centauri B formed at the same time from a common collection of matter.* As the question suggests, stars that form from the same collection of matter have similar chemical compositions. Therefore, Student 2 would likely suggest that Alpha Centauri A and Alpha Centauri B have similar chemical compositions because they formed *from a common collection of matter*. Alpha Centauri C formed from a different collection of matter, eliminating choices (G), (H), and (J). Only choice (F) remains.

31. **C** The introduction to this passage contains the following information: *Alpha Centauri A, a 1.10-solar-mass yellow dwarf star, where one solar mass unit is equivalent to the mass of the Sun.* The question states that the mass of the Sun is 2.0×10^{33} g. Therefore, the mass of Alpha Centauri A must be 1.10 times this value, given the definition of solar mass. Don't worry about calculating the exact value: You know that this value must be slightly greater than the mass of the sun, and only choice (C) gives a value greater than 2.0×10^{33} g.

32. **J** Use POE. This question requires a bit of outside knowledge, but it can be solved easily with a bit of common sense. First of all, Fact 2 states that the nuclei being fused are *composed of protons*. It is therefore not likely that the answer to this question will have anything to do with *electrons*, eliminating choices (F) and (G). *Helium fusion* describes the process by which these protons are *fused*, or put together. Think about it this way: If these protons are attracted to each other to begin with, do you think it would take a bunch of extra energy to put them together? Not likely! Eliminate choice (H), and only choice (J) remains.

33. **C** Fact 5 contains the following information: Red dwarves are smaller stars that can also carry out helium fusion. These stars can develop into white dwarves sooner than yellow and orange dwarves. Student 1 states, *The large Alpha Centauri C had more helium fusion than the other two stars, so it quickly became the smallest of the stars.* Therefore, according to this information, Alpha Centauri C is one of those smaller stars that can develop into white dwarves sooner. Choice (C) is our best answer. Also, Scientist 1 doesn't ever really talk about any differences between Alpha Centauri A and Alpha Centauri B, so it's unlikely that one would be correct and the other incorrect.

34. **J** Use POE. If you're not sure how to answer "Yes" or "No," look at the reasons. Student 2's hypothesis contains the following information: *Alpha Centauri A was initially more massive than Alpha Centauri B.* This eliminates choices (F) and (H) immediately. Fact 5 contains the following information: *Red dwarves are smaller stars that can also carry out helium fusion. These stars can develop into white dwarves sooner than yellow and orange dwarves.* Therefore, since Alpha Centauri B is smaller, it is one of the *smaller stars* that *can develop into white dwarves sooner*. Therefore, it is not likely that it will spend the same amount of time as a white dwarf. Think about it this way: Fact 5 suggests that the main qualification for a *white dwarf* is its size. If Student 2 is correct about Alpha Centauri A and Alpha Centauri B having different sizes, their *white dwarf* qualifications can't be the same, so eliminate choice (G).

Passage VII

35. D The words *magnetic field strength* don't appear explicitly in the question, but they are suggested by the word *attract*. Therefore, use Figure 2 to figure out the relationship between the number of coils and the magnetic field strength. According to this Figure, the magnetic field strength increases with increasing number of coils for all three curves shown. Therefore, in order to get the strongest possible magnetic field, we will need the maximum number of coils, or 200, as in choice (D).

36. J Use POE. If you're not sure whether to answer "Yes" or "No," check the reasons. The variable l_0 appears on the *x*-axis of Figure 3 at a single point: solenoid length of 0.1 m. This point does stays the same, regardless of the other variables, eliminating choices (F) and (H). Then, l_0 cannot be said to vary with any of the variables on this Figure, including μ, eliminating choice (G). Only choice (J) remains.

37. B Find $\mu = 14 \times 10^{-5}$ in the key for Figure 3. Notice, though, that all three of these curves follow the same trend: as solenoid length increases, L decreases and then levels off at the end. Only choice (B) offers an answer choice consistent with this information.

38. J According to Figure 3, as solenoid length increases, L decreases. The μ curves don't follow quite so consistent a relationship. Pick a point and see how these μ values relate to one another. At a solenoid length of 0.2 m, the μ value associated with the largest L value is $\mu = 28 \times 10^{-5}$. The μ value associated with the smallest L value is $\mu = 7 \times 10^{-5}$. Therefore, the correct answer should have 28×10^{-5} as its first value and 7×10^{-5} as its last. Only choice (J) works.

39. B According to the passage, *the* average minimum solenoid length, l_o, *for a solenoid containing 100 coils was determined*. Therefore, we need to determine the value of l_0. According to Figure 3, l_0 appears on the *x*-axis at solenoid length 0.1 m. Only choice (B) works.

Later Passages

Passage I

In an experimental device known as a *cloud chamber*, protons and electrons act as *condensation nuclei* that get ionized by alcohol vapor inside the chamber to form a *high-energy mist*. When this mist acquires enough energy, it forms *tracks* that travel through the chamber. These tracks can then be accelerated when exposed to a magnetic field; with protons and electrons moving in opposite directions.

Two studies using cloud chambers were done at a research center in a temperate climate, using supercooled gaseous ethanol as a medium. The cloud chamber temperature ranged from 0°C to –150°C.

Study 1

Four types of anions (A–D) were used. Anions of each type, when released into the cloud chamber, emit groups of electrons into the chamber with a specific distribution of charges (see Table 1).

Table 1				
Anion Type	Percent of groups of electrons having charges (coulombs):			
	0.1–0.5	0.6–1.0	1.1–1.5	1.5–2.0
A	70	20	8	2
B	75	10	8	7
C	80	8	7	5
D	85	7	5	3
1 coulomb is the charge of 6.24×10^{18} electrons.				

A device containing all 4 types of anions was placed next to the cloud chamber. A computer in the device determined whether or not to immediately release at least 1 anion, emitting electrons into the chamber. The computer also selected which type of anion to release, and how many anions to release to generate 10, 100, 1,000, or 10,000 condensation nuclei per cm^3 within the chamber. The average number of tracks produced by each type of anion and at each concentration of condensation nuclei is shown in Figure 1.

concentration of condensation nuclei
(nuclei/cubic centimeter)

Figure 1

Study 2

The magnetic force required to make each track to accelerate away from a straight line was recorded over an hour following the release of the four types of anions into two types of cloud chambers: one with ethanol vapor and one with water vapor. The averaged results for both types of cloud chambers are shown in Figure 2.

time after release of anions (minutes)

Figure 2

1. According to the results of Study 1, as the condensation nuclei concentration increased, the average number of tracks generated:

   A. increased for all 4 types of anions.
   B. increased for anion types A and B, but decreased for anion types C and D.
   C. decreased for all 4 types of anions.
   D. decreased for anion types A and B, but increased for anion types C and D.

2. Based on the passage, what is the correct order of tracks, subatomic particles, and condensation nuclei, according to their diameters, from smallest to largest?

   F. Subatomic particle, track, condensation nucleus
   G. Subatomic particle, condensation nucleus, track
   H. Track, subatomic particle, condensation nucleus
   J. Track, condensation nucleus, subatomic particle

3. According to the results of Study 2, how did the magnetic fields required in the cloud chamber with ethanol vapor differ from the magnetic fields required in the cloud chamber with water vapor with respect to their maximum strength?

A. It took more time for the magnetic field in the ethanol vapor to reach a maximum strength, and it reached a greater maximum strength.

B. It took less time for the magnetic field in the ethanol vapor to reach a maximum strength, and it reached a greater maximum strength.

C. It took more time for the magnetic field in the ethanol vapor to reach a maximum strength, and it reached a lesser maximum strength.

D. It took less time for the magnetic field in the ethanol vapor to reach a maximum strength, and it reached a lesser maximum strength.

4. The design of Study 1 differed from the design of Study 2 in that Study 1, the:

F. tracks of condensation nuclei were analyzed, whereas in Study 2, the concentration of condensation nuclei was analyzed.

G. strength of magnetic fields was measured, whereas in Study 2, the concentration of condensation nuclei was analyzed.

H. tracks of condensation nuclei were analyzed, whereas in Study 2, the strength of magnetic fields was analyzed.

J. strength of magnetic fields was analyzed, whereas in Study 2, tracks of condensation nuclei were analyzed.

5. Which of the following statements gives the most likely reason that data from the cloud chamber was not recorded below a temperature of −150°C? Below −150°C, there would be present:

A. only water vapor.
B. only alcohol vapor.
C. ice crystals but little water vapor.
D. solidified alcohol but little alcohol vapor.

6. Which of the following statements about the concentration of condensation nuclei in the 4 types of anions is supported by Table 1 ?

F. For all 4 types of anions, the majority of particles belonged to the largest charge category.

G. For all 4 types of anions, the majority of particles belong to the smallest charge category.

H. For anion types A and B, most anions belong to the largest charge category, whereas for anion types C and D, most anions belong to the smallest charge category.

J. For anion types A and B, most anions belong to the smallest charge category, whereas for anion types C and D, most anions belong to the largest charge category.

Passage II

Three experiments were conducted using the gases nitrogen (N_2), nitrogen dioxide (NO_2), and xenon (Xe). For each gas:

1. A cap was placed on a 2 L metal chamber, containing sensors to measure temperature and pressure and a vale to allow gas to enter.

2. Air was pumped out of the chamber until the pressure inside was measured to be 0.00 mmHg.

3. The chamber was placed on an analytical balance, which was then reset to 0.00 g.

4. Some of the gas was added to the chamber.

5. When the gas in the vessel reached room temperature (298 K), the mass and pressure inside were recorded.

6. Steps 4 and 5 were repeated for different masses.

The experiments were repeated using a 4 L metal chamber (see Figures 1 and 2).

mass of gas (g)

Figure 1

mass of gas (g)

Figure 2

7. Based on Figure 2, if 12 g of Xe had been added to the 4 L vessel, the pressure would have been:

   A. less than 300 mmHg.
   B. between 300 and 600 mmHg.
   C. between 600 mmHg and 900 mmHg.
   D. greater than 1200 mmHg.

8. Suppose the experiments had been repeated, except with a 3 L vessel. Based on Figures 1 and 2, the pressure exerted by 10 g of NO_2 would most likely have been:

   F. less than 1000 mmHg.
   G. between 1000 and 2000 mmHg.
   H. between 2000 and 2500 mmHg.
   J. greater than 2500 mmHg.

9. Based on Figures 1 and 2, for a given mass of N_2 at 298 K, how does the pressure exerted by the N_2 in a 4 L vessel compare to the pressure exerted by the N_2 in a 2 L vessel? In the 4 L vessel, the N_2 pressure will be:

   A. half as great as in the 2 L vessel.
   B. the same as in the 2 L vessel.
   C. twice as great as in the 2 L vessel.
   D. 4 times as great as in the 2 L vessel.

10. Which of the following best explains why equal masses of N_2 and NO_2 at the same temperature and in vessels of similar sizes had different pressures? The pressure exerted by the N_2 was:

F. greater, because there were fewer N_2 molecules per gram than there were NO_2 molecules per gram.

G. greater, because there were more N_2 molecules per gram than there were NO_2 molecules per gram.

H. less, because there were fewer N_2 molecules per gram than there were NO_2 molecules per gram.

J. less, because there were more N_2 molecules per gram than there were NO_2 molecules per gram.

11. Suppose the experiment involving N_2 and the 4 L vessel had been repeated, except at a temperature of 287 K. For a given mass of N_2, compared to the pressure measured in the original experiment, the pressure measured at 287 K would have been:

A. greater, because pressure is directly proportional to temperature.

B. greater, because pressure is inversely proportional to temperature.

C. less, because pressure is directly proportional to temperature.

D. less, because pressure is inversely proportional to temperature.

Passage III

Escherichia coli (E. coli) are commonly used in laboratories for the expression, replication, and purification of introduced circular pieces of DNA called *plasmids*. Engineered plasmids encode a gene of interest and often genes that confer resistances to select antibiotics. Antibiotic resistance may be analyzed using the *disk diffusion method*. During the disk diffusion method, bacteria from a single *colony*, or a cluster of genetically identical cells, are incubated in liquid growth media and spread on agar plates (see Figure 1). Small paper disks containing a known concentration of antibiotic are set on the agar plates and the bacteria are allowed to grow at optimal temperatures. Laboratory strains of *E. coli* lacking plasmids containing genes of resistance to select antibiotics will be unable to grow near the disk containing that antibiotic. Only bacteria that have received the introduced plasmid containing an antibiotic resistance gene should be able to grow in the presence of the antibiotic-containing disk.

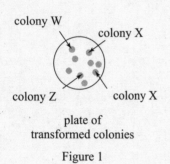

colony W

colony X

colony Z

colony X

plate of
transformed colonies

Figure 1

Experiment 1

A biotech company has engineered new laboratory strains (A–E) of *E. coli* and is testing whether each strain could grow in the presence of a variety of common antibiotics—ampicillin (Amp), kanamycin (Kan), penicillin (Pen), and tetracycline (Tet). Each of the strains was incubated in a clear nutrient media containing either extra sugar (glucose) or an antibiotic at 37°C for 24 hr. After 24 hrs, the growth media was examined for *turbidity* or cloudiness, a signal of bacterial growth (see Table 1).

Strain	Nutrient Media				
	+Glu	+Amp	+Kan	+Pen	+Tet
A	+	+	−	+	−
B	+	−	−	+	−
C	+	−	−	+	+
D	+	+	+	−	−
E	+	−	+	+	−

Table 1

Note: + indicates presence of turbidity;
− indicates no change in appearance

Experiment 2

The scientists at the biotech company tested strain B for growth after *transformation*, a process of introducing engineered plasmids, with antibiotic-resistance containing plasmids. Four different transformed colonies (W, X, Y, and Z) and untransformed strain B were incubated in liquid growth media and spread on agar plates. To identify which colonies had received which resistance genes, disks containing one of each of the common antibiotics were then placed on the agar plate and the bacteria were permitted to grow at 37°C (see Figure 2).

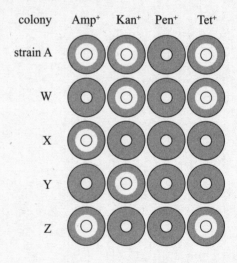

Figure 2

12. Suppose *E. coli* Strain D had been incubated on plates containing kanamycin and tetracycline (Kan⁺Tet⁺) disks and growth near both disks was observed. Do the data in Table 1 support this observation?

F. Yes; the results shown in Table 1 indicate that Strain D can grow in the presence of both Kan and Tet.

G. Yes; the results shown in Table 1 indicate that Strain D cannot grow in the presence of Kan.

H. No; the results shown in Table 1 indicate that Strain D can grow in the presence of both Kan and Tet.

J. No; the results shown in Table 1 indicate that Strain D cannot grow in the presence of Tet.

13. Which of the labeled colonies shown in Figure 2 is most likely to have received a plasmid containing resistance to tetracycline?

A. Colonies W and X
B. Colonies X and Z
C. Colonies Y and Z
D. Colonies X and Y

14. According to Table 1, how many strains tested in Experiment 1 were able to grow in nutrient media containing penicillin?

F. 0
G. 1
H. 2
J. 4

15. Based on Table 1 and Figure 2, which colonies, if any, likely received a plasmid with resistance genes to ampicillin and tetracycline?

A. Colony W only
B. Colony Y only
C. Colonies X and Y
D. Colonies Y and Z

16. Before beginning the experiments, the scientists sprayed the lab area down with a disinfectant. The most likely reason that the disinfectant was used was to avoid contaminating:

F. the nutrient growth media with strains that were lab generated.

G. the agar plates with strains that were lab generated.

H. both the nutrient growth media and agar plates with strains that were lab generated.

J. both the nutrient growth media and agar plates with strains that were not lab generated.

17. Which of the colonies shown in Figure 2 did NOT grow in the presence of penicillin?

A. Colony X
B. Colony Y
C. Colony Z
D. None of the strains

Passage IV

The *absolute threshold pressure for hearing* is the minimum air pressure at each audio frequency that can produce a sound that is detectable by the human ear. The *pain threshold pressure for hearing* is the maximum air pressure at each frequency that the human ear can withstand without sensing pain.

Figure 1 below displays the absolute and pain threshold pressures for hearing in two media: air and water. The figure also shows P, the percentage increase in compression of the air or water with increasing sound pressure. Audio frequency is given in cycles per second (cyc/sec), and sound pressure level is given in decibels (db).

Figure 1

18. According to the figure, which of the following is the closest to the highest frequency that can be heard by a human being?

    F. 1 cyc/sec
    G. 10 cyc/sec
    H. 100 cyc/sec
    J. 1000 cyc/sec

19. Based on the figure, a sound of a given frequency will have the highest sound level pressure for which of the following sets of conditions?

    Sound in: P

    A. Air $10^{-8}\%$
    B. Air $10^{-1}\%$
    C. Water $10^{-8}\%$
    D. Water $10^{-1}\%$

20. As humans grow older, there is often a loss in the ability to hear sounds at high frequencies. Which of the following figures best illustrates this?

21. A scientist developed a hypothesis that sounds with any sound pressure level would be painful to humans if the frequency were 10^4 cyc/sec. Do the data from the figure support this hypothesis?

A. No, because humans are unable to hear sounds over 10^4 cyc/sec.

B. No, because the absolute threshold of pain for hearing is relatively constant with changes in frequency.

C. Yes, because the absolute threshold of pain for hearing is relatively constant with changes in frequency.

D. Yes, because as frequency increases above 10^4 cyc/sec, the absolute threshold of pain for hearing also increases.

22. Based on the figure, does P depend on the frequency of sound at a given sound pressure level?

F. No, because as frequency increases, P increases.

G. No, because as frequency increases, P remains constant.

H. Yes, because as frequency increases, P increases.

J. Yes, because as frequency increases, P remains constant.

Passage V

A group of students added 100 mg of Salt A to an Erlenmeyer flask containing 100 mL of water at 20°C. The mixture was heated over a *Bunsen burner* and a thermometer placed in the flask to acquire temperature readings (Figure 1).

Figure 1

The mixture was heated and temperature readings acquired every 30 sec until the solution reached a full boil and the solid had completely dissolved. The boiling temperature for the solution was measured to be 104°C. The procedure was repeated with Salt B, which resulted in a boiling temperature of 110°C.

The teacher asked 3 of the students in the group to explain why the solutions had different boiling temperatures.

Student 1

The solution containing Salt B had a higher boiling point because Salt B produces more ions in solution than Salt A. As the solid dissolves, the salt ionizes and interacts with water molecules. This causes more interactions between the ions and water thus requiring more energy for water molecules to break these interactions and become a gas (boiling). Since salts become ions in solution, salts that produce more ions will have more interactions with water than salts producing fewer ions. Thus, if two salts of equal amounts are added to water, the solution containing the salt that produces more ions will boil at the higher temperature.

Student 2

The solution containing Salt B had a higher boiling point because it had a lower *molar mass* (the mass of 6.02×10^{23} particles). Consider equal amounts of two salts with different molar masses. More mass is required of the salt with the greater molar mass to result in the same number of particles. Since more heat energy is required to boil water with more interactions, the solution with more salt particles will boil at a higher temperature. Thus, if equal amounts of two salts with different molar masses are added, the salt with the lower molar mass will result in more particles and a greater solution boiling point than a salt with a greater molar mass.

Student 3

The solution containing Salt B had a higher boiling point because Salt B releases more heat upon dissolving than Salt A. The *enthalpy change of dissolution* ($\Delta H°_{diss}$) is a measure of the net amount of heat energy absorbed in the process of dissolving a salt. Salts that absorb more energy to dissolve will have more positive $\Delta H°_{diss}$ values and will make the solution cooler. Salts that absorb less energy than they release will have more negative $\Delta H°_{diss}$ values and will make the solution warmer. If equal amounts of two salts with different $\Delta H°_{diss}$ values are dissolved in solution, the solution containing the salt with the more negative $\Delta H°_{diss}$ value will release more heat and thus result in a greater boiling point.

The number of ions produced, molar mass, and enthalpy change dissolution ($\Delta H°_{diss}$) of some common salts are shown in Table 1.

Table 1			
Salt	Ions Produced	Molar Mass (g/mol)	$\Delta H°_{diss}$ (kJ/mol)
Sodium chloride	2	58.4	+ 3.9
Calcium chloride	3	111.0	− 81.2
Ammonium nitrate	2	80.1	+ 25.7
Potassium hydroxide	2	56.11	− 57.6
Magnesium sulfate	2	120.38	− 91.0

23. Suppose that Salt A had been potassium hydroxide and Salt B had been magnesium sulfate. The results of the experiment would have supported the explanation(s) provided by which student(s)?

   A. Student 2 only
   B. Student 3 only
   C. Students 1 and 3 only
   D. Students 2 and 3 only

24. Suppose that the students also tested ammonium nitrate in the experiment and found it to have resulted in a boiling temperature in solution of 107°C. Student 2 would claim that ammonium nitrate:

   F. has a greater molar mass than Salt A, but a smaller molar mass than Salt B.
   G. has a greater molar mass than Salt B, but a smaller molar mass than Salt A.
   H. has a greater enthalpy change of dissolution than Salt A, but a smaller enthalpy change of dissolution than Salt B.
   J. has a greater enthalpy change of dissolution than Salt B, but a smaller enthalpy change of dissolution than Salt A.

25. Which of the following graphs of the relative number of particles produced is most consistent with Student 2's explanation?

A.

B.

C.

D.

26. During the experiment, the temperature reading in the thermometer as readings were taken every 30 sec:

F. increased only.
G. decreased only.
H. increased, then decreased.
J. decreased, then increased.

27. Based on Student 3's explanation, which of the salts in Table 1 would result in the greatest solution boiling temperature?

A. Calcium chloride
B. Ammonium nitrate
C. Potassium hydroxide
D. Magnesium sulfate

28. Consider the data for cesium hydroxide shown in the table below:

Ions Produced	Molar Mass (g/mol)	ΔH°_{diss} (kJ/mol)
2	149.91	−71.6

Which student(s), if any, would predict that cesium hydroxide would produce a solution with a lower boiling temperature than calcium chloride?

F. Student 1 only
G. Students 2 and 3 only
H. Students 1, 2, and 3
J. None of the students

29. Is the claim "If equal amounts of salt are dissolved, sodium chloride will result in a greater boiling point than ammonium nitrate" consistent with Student 2's explanation?

A. No, because sodium chloride has a smaller molar mass than ammonium nitrate.
B. No, because sodium chloride has a more negative enthalpy change of dissolution.
C. Yes, because sodium chloride has a smaller molar mass than ammonium nitrate.
D. Yes, because sodium chloride has a more negative enthalpy change of dissolution.

Ions in seawater, such as Cl^-, SO_4^{2-}, Na^+, and Mg^{2+}, are carried down to the ocean floor through a process known as *marine deposition*. SO_4^{2-} and Mg^{2+} primarily come from the erosion of rocks, while Cl^- and Na^+ come from both mineral erosion and underwater volcanoes and hydrothermal vents.

Study 1

A fluid motion sensor was placed on a section of the seabed in the Atlantic Ocean, and data were collected over 12 months. At 6:00 a.m. every morning, the movement of water past the sensor was recorded, and a small amount of water was sequestered. Figure 1 shows the water movement that was measured in m^3 per second.

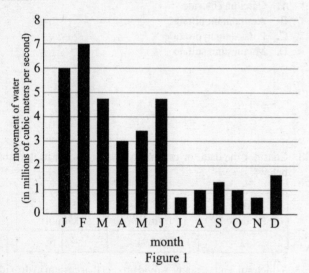

month

Figure 1

At the end of each month, the sequestered water was extracted by a science research crew, and a portion was analyzed for the concentrations of Cl^- and SO_4^{2-} ions. Using these data, the marine deposition was measured in kilograms (kg) per cubic meter (m^3) for each substance in each month (see Figure 2).

month

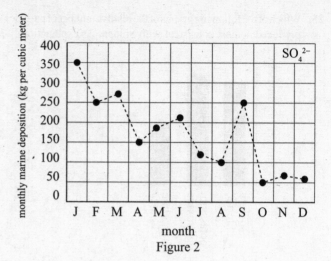

month

Figure 2

Study 2

Another portion of the monthly water sample was analyzed for concentrations of Na^+ and Mg^{2+} ions. The monthly marine deposition was calculated for each substance in equivalents (Eq) per m^3 (see Figure 3).

month

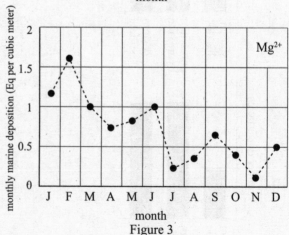

month

Figure 3

Study 3

The annual marine deposition of Cl^- and SO_4^{2-} ions over the 12-month period was calculated in kg/m³ at the test site, and also at two sites in the Arctic Ocean, located 2,000 and 4,000 miles north, respectively (see Figure 4).

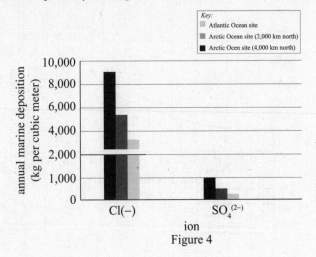

Figure 4

30. According to Figure 1, during the year over which data were collected, the movement of water was greatest in February and least in November. According to Figures 2 and 3, the marine deposition of which ion was also greatest in February and least in November?

F. Cl^-
G. Mg^{2+}
H. Na^+
J. SO_4^{2-}

31. Based on the results from Study 1, the mean monthly marine deposition for Cl^- over the year of the study was:

A. less than 900 kg/m³.
B. between 900 kg/m³ and 1,000 kg/m³.
C. between 1,000 kg/m³ and 1,200 kg/m³.
D. over 1,200 kg/m³.

32. A student states, "The marine deposition of Na^+ is highest in the winter and lowest in the summer, since the winter features greater activity of volcanoes and hydrothermal vents." Is this statement supported by the results of Study 2 ?

F. No, because marine deposition of Na^+ was, on average, greater between November and January than it was between June and August.
G. No, because marine deposition of Na^+ was, on average, less between November and January than it was between June and August.
H. Yes, because marine deposition of Na^+ was, on average, greater between November and January than it was between June and August.
J. Yes, because marine deposition of Na^+ was, on average, less between November and January than it was between June and August.

33. Suppose that the fluid motion sensor was placed in an underwater cave in the Atlantic Ocean where there is no net movement of water during one month of the 12-month study. The information provided indicates that during that month, there would have been:

A. no marine deposition of any of the 4 substances.
B. no marine deposition of Cl^- and SO_4^{2-}, but a high level of marine deposition of Na+ and Mg^{2+}.
C. high marine deposition of Cl^- and SO_4^{2-}, but no marine deposition of Na+ and Mg^{2+}.
D. high marine deposition of all 4 substances.

34. According to Study 3, as the distance from the fluid motion sensor in the Atlantic Ocean decreased, the annual marine deposition:

F. decreased for both Cl^- and SO_4^{2-}.
G. decreased for Cl^- but increased for SO_4^{2-}.
H. increased for Cl^- but decreased for SO_4^{2-}.
J. increased for both Cl^- and SO_4^{2-}.

35. Which of the following variables remained constant in Study 2 ?

A. Marine deposition of SO_4^{2-}
B. Marine deposition of Mg^{2+}
C. Movement of water during the month
D. Location of the study

Passage VII

Oxidation-reduction titration is a method in which precise volumes of a *titrant* (an oxidizing or reducing agent) are added dropwise to a known volume of an *analyte* (a reducing or oxidizing agent, respectively). This process can be monitored by adding a *redox indicator* (a substance that changes color over a certain range of electrode potentials) to the analyte or by measuring the sample's *voltage* using a potentiometer. Voltage (measured in kilovolts, kV) is a measure of the force of an electrical current that could be transmitted by the solution.

Two titration experiments were performed at 298 K using a 0.10 M iodine (I_2) solution and either a 0.0010 M sulfur dioxide (SO_2) solution or a 0.0010 M sodium thiosulfate solution (where M is the number of moles of oxidizing or reducing agent per liter of solution). All solutions were aqueous. A redox indicator solution of *starch* was also used. Starch and I_2 form a complex with a deep blue color, but when I_2 is reduced to 2 iodide (I^-) ions, the complex dissipates and the solution becomes colorless.

Experiment 1

A drop of starch solution was added to an Erlenmeyer flask containing 100.0 mL of the SO_2 solution. A potentiometer, which acts as a control input for electronic circuits, was placed in the solution. The I_2 solution was incrementally added to the SO_2 solution. After each addition, the SO_2 solution was stirred and the solution's color and voltage were recorded (see Figure 1).

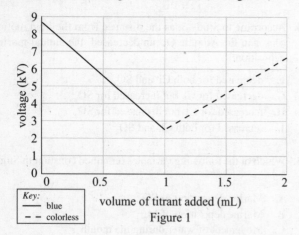

Figure 1

Experiment 2

Experiment 1 was repeated, except that the sodium thiosulfate solution was used instead of the SO_2 solution (see Figure 2).

Figure 2

36. In Experiment 1, the analyte was blue at which of the following volumes of titrant added?

F. 0.7 mL
G. 1.1 mL
H. 1.5 mL
J. 1.9 mL

37. In Experiment 2, the analyte was in its reduced form for which of the following volumes of titrant added?

A. 0.3 mL
B. 0.6 mL
C. 0.9 mL
D. 1.2 mL

38. In Experiment 1, if 2.5 mL of titrant was added to the analyte, the voltage would most likely have been:

F. less than 1 kV.
G. between 1 kV and 4 kV.
H. between 4 kV and 7 kV.
J. more than 7 kV.

39. In Experiment 2, which solution was the analyte and which solution was the titrant?

titrant	sample solution
A. Sodium thiosulfate	I
B. SO_2	I_2
C. I_2	Sodium thiosulfate
D. I_2	SO_2

40. In Experiments 1 and 2, the potentiometer that was placed in the analyte most likely did which of the following?

F. Detected the concentration of starch in the solution

G. Conducted an electric current initiated by ions in the solution

H. Heated the solution to its boiling point

J. Cooled to solution to its freezing point

41. A chemist states that in Experiment 2, the analyte was fully reduced with 0.2 mL of titrant added, but not with 1.8 mL of titrant added. Do the results of Experiment 2 support this claim?

A. Yes; at a value of 0.2 mL of titrant added, the analyte was blue, while at a value of 1.8 mL of titrant added, the analyte was colorless.

B. Yes; at a value of 0.2 mL of titrant added, the analyte was colorless, while at a value of 1.8 mL of titrant added, the analyte was blue.

C. No; at a value of 0.2 mL of titrant added, the analyte was blue, while at a value of 1.8 mL of titrant added, the analyte was colorless.

D. No; at a value of 0.2 mL of titrant added, the analyte was colorless, while at a value of 1.8 mL of titrant added, the analyte was blue.

ANSWERS

Passage I

1. C
2. G
3. C
4. H
5. D
6. G

Passage II

7. B
8. G
9. A
10. G
11. C

Passage III

12. J
13. D
14. J
15. B
16. J
17. D

Passage IV

18. J
19. D
20. G
21. A
22. G

Passage V

23. B
24. G
25. A
26. F
27. D
28. H
29. C

Passage VI

30. G
31. B
32. H
33. A
34. J
35. D

Passage VII

36. F
37. D
38. J
39. C
40. G
41. C

EXPLANATIONS

Passage I

1. **C** In Figure 1, all four anions follow the same trend, so eliminate choices (B) and (D) immediately. From left to right in the graph, the concentration of condensation nuclei is increasing for all four anions, and as this value increases, the average number of tracks decreases for all four anions. Only choice (C) accurately reflects this trend.

2. **G** The first paragraph states the following: *protons and electrons act as condensation nuclei that get ionized by alcohol vapor inside the chamber to form a high-energy mist. When this mist acquires enough energy, it forms tracks that travel through the chamber.* Since tracks form the last part of the process, it can be inferred that they are made from the other two parts, and therefore the largest of the three. Only choice (G) offers an answer choice that correctly places tracks as the largest of the three components.

3. **C** Notice from the answer choices that this question has two components: time to maximum magnetic force and maximum magnetic force itself. Notice also that all the answer choices focus on the *ethanol vapor*. According to Figure 2, the ethanol vapor took about 40 minutes to reach its maximum magnetic field where the water vapor took only about 15 minutes. Therefore, the ethanol vapor took more time, eliminating choices (B) and (D). The ethanol vapor reached a maximum magnetic field of approximately 4.25 Newtons, where the water vapor reached a maximum magnetic field of approximately 4.75 Newtons. Therefore, the ethanol vapor's magnetic field reached a lesser maximum strength, eliminating choice (A) and making choice (C) the correct answer.

4. **H** Note the axes on each of the graphs. "Magnetic field" appears only in Study 2, which eliminates choices (G) and (J) immediately. Then, since magnetic field is the primary focus of Study 2, eliminate choice (F) because it contains no mention of magnetic field. Only choice (H) remains and contains accurate information regarding both studies.

5. **D** This requires a bit of logical thinking and some outside knowledge. Only Study 2 is concerned with *water vapor*, whereas the general introduction discusses *alcohol vapor*. Therefore, it can be inferred that the entire experiment deals with *alcohol vapor*, making changes in water vapor only partially relevant, eliminating choices (A) and (C). Then, between the two answer choices, which is more likely to be the case at temperatures *below* –150°C? Alcohol in this temperature range is colder and therefore more likely to be solid than vapor. Only choice (D) reflects this information correctly.

6. **G** According to Table 1, 75–80% of all four types of anions fit in to the 0.1–0.5 category, or the "smallest charge category." There are no exceptions in Table 1, so the only answer choice that can work is choice (G).

Passage II

7. B   Figure 2 only gives the information up to 10 g of gas added, but fortunately, all these curves have a very consistent relationship: As mass of gas goes up, the pressure goes up. In the 4 L vessel, when 10 g of Xe is added, the pressure is approximately 300 mmHg. At 12 g of Xe, the pressure should be slightly higher, somewhere around 450 mmHg. Only choice (B) gives a range that contains this value.

8. G   As you compare Figures 1 and 2, notice how much higher the pressure values are in Figure 1. It can therefore be assumed that the 2 L vessel has higher pressure values than the 4 L vessel, shown in Figure 2. The pressure values in a 3 L vessel should therefore be greater than those of the 4 L vessel but less than those of the 2 L vessel. In the 2 L vessel, 10 g of NO_2 gives a pressure of approximately 2000 mmHg. In the 4 L vessel, 10 g of NO_2 gives a pressure of approximately 1000 mmHg. Therefore, in a 3 L vessel, 10 g of NO_2 should give a pressure between 1000 and 2000 mmHg, as in choice (G).

9. A   There's a new value in this problem, but as Step 5 of the introduction indicates, *298 K* is merely the temperature at which the mass and pressure were recorded. It is therefore already implied in Figures 1 and 2, so you don't have to worry about it. Since we need to compare the N_2 values from Figures 1 and 2, it's best to find values as exact as possible. Notice that at mass 6 g, the 2 L vessel has a pressure of 2000 mmHg, and the 4 L vessel has a pressure of 1000 mmHg. Therefore, the pressure in the 4 L vessel is *half as great as* the pressure in the 2 L vessel. Only choice (A) works.

10. G   Use POE. In Figures 1 and 2, the pressure when N_2 is used is consistently greater than the pressure when the NO_2 is used. Eliminate choices (H) and (J). Then, you'll need a bit of outside knowledge to complete the question. Simply stated, an N_2 molecule has fewer components than an NO_2 molecule, so it has a smaller mass. Therefore, in order to get the same mass of both molecules, we will need more N_2 molecules per gram, eliminating choice (F).

11. C   This question requires a bit of outside knowledge. You need to know the relationship between pressure and temperature: As pressure increases, so does temperature. This is a *direct* relationship, eliminating choices (B) and (D). Because of this relationship, as the temperature decreases from 298 K to 287 K, the pressure will decrease also, as in choice (C).

Passage III

12. J   Use POE. If you're not sure whether to answer "Yes" or "No," check the reasons. According to Table 1, Strain D can grow in the presence of Glu, Amp, and Kan. Eliminate choice (G), which states that Strain D cannot grow in the presence of Kan. Also according to Table 1, Strain D cannot grow in the presence of Pen or Tet. Eliminate choices (F) and (H), which suggest that Strain D can grow in the presence of Tet. Only choice (J) remains.

13. D   The question says that you only need Figure 2, but the presence of Strain A at the top of the figure links the figure back to Figure 1. According to Figure 1, Strain A can grow in the presence of Glu, Amp, and Pen. It cannot grow in the presence of Kan or Tet. It can be inferred that if a colony *can* grow in the presence of one of these substances, the colony pictured will have a larger white region. Therefore, the colonies that have received a "plasmid containing resistance to tetracycline" should have a smaller white region in the "Tet" column. Colonies X and Y have this small white region, making choice (D) the best answer.

14. J   According to Table 1, Strains A, B, C, and E were able to grow in the presence of penicillin, or "+Pen." Choice (J) gives the correct number.

15. B   According to Figure 1, Strain A can grow in the presence of Glu, Amp, and Pen. It cannot grow in the presence of Kan or Tet. It can be inferred that if a colony *can* grow in the presence of one of these substances, the colony pictured will have a larger white region. Therefore, the colonies that have received a plasmid "with resistance genes to ampicillin and tetracycline" should have a smaller white region in the Amp and Tet columns. Only Strain Y shows a resistance to *both* substances, making choice (B) the only acceptable answer.

16. J   This question requires a bit of outside knowledge about why scientists do what they do when setting up experiments. Use POE and common sense. Notice choices (F), (G), and (H) all contain mention of substances that are "lab generated." Only choice (J) contains mention of strains that are "not lab generated." Think about it this way: Scientists are trying to control the environment of their experiment, so they don't want things from outside (things that are "not lab generated") to contaminate the things in the experiment. Also, notice that choices (H) and (J) are direct opposites, a good indication that one of them will be correct.

17. D   According to Figure 1, Strain A can grow in the presence of Glu, Amp, and Pen. It cannot grow in the presence of Kan or Tet. It can be inferred that if a colony *can* grow in the presence of one of these substances, the colony pictured will have a larger white region. None of the strains in Figure 2 have this large white region under "Pen+," suggesting that none of them are able to grow in the presence of penicillin, making choice (D) the correct answer. Also, notice that all the colonies in the "Pen+" column look the same. Therefore, they're clearly not acting any differently from one another in the presence of this substance, so the only possible answer is (D).

Passage IV

18. J   The first line of the passage states the following: The absolute threshold pressure for hearing is the minimum air pressure at each audio frequency that can produce a sound that is detectable by the human ear. In other words, the absolute threshold pressure for hearing gives the highest pressure and frequency at which humans can hear. In order to answer this question, we'll need to use Figure 1 and the curve labeled "Absolute pressure threshold for hearing," and we will need to find its maximum frequency, listed on the x-axis. According to Figure 1, this curve maxes out right around 1×10^3 cyc/sec, or 1000 cyc/sec, as in choice (J). If you selected choice (H) be careful, this is the point of minimum Sound Pressure Level, not the maximum frequency.

19. D   Use POE. Note the key at the bottom of Figure 1. According to this key, "Water" is shown on the graph with a solid line, and "Air" is shown on the graph with a dotted line. The solid line is consistently higher than the dotted, suggesting that "Water" can withstand higher frequencies, eliminating choices (A) and (B). Then, note the P-values on the right side of the graph. According to the graph, these P-values increase with increasing sound pressure level, so in order to increase the sound pressure level, we will want the highest possible P-value, which in the list of remaining answer choices is 10^{-1}%, as in choice (D).

20. G   Use POE. According to this question, some change happens at high frequencies. Accordingly, whichever graph we choose will need to show a change at high frequency, rather than low frequency. Based on this information alone, we can eliminate choices (F) and (H). Then, the dotted curve ("After hearing loss") should indicate some kind of hearing *loss* at high frequencies, so it should show a curve that does not quite reach the highest frequencies, as only choice (G) does. If you selected choice (J), you may have reversed the two curves.

21. A   The frequency of 10^4 cyc/sec doesn't appear on the graph, but according to Figure 1, the absolute threshold of hearing is around 10^3 cyc/sec. The pain threshold of hearing is within the absolute threshold, so if 10^4 cyc/sec isn't within the absolute threshold, it won't be within the pain threshold either. Think of it this way: In order for something to hurt when you hear it, you need to be able to hear it first. Therefore, only choice (A) can work because it is the only answer choice with a reason consistent with the information in Figure 1.

22. G   Use POE. If you're unsure whether to answer "Yes" or "No," check the reasons. Use Figure 1. Frequency appears on the x-axis, and Pressure appears on the y-axis. According to the lines showing the pressure "in Air" and "in Water," the increasing frequency has no effect on the pressure values. Eliminate choices (F) and (H). Therefore, the pressure does *not* depend on the frequency, making choice (G) the correct answer.

Passage V

23. **B** According to Table 1, potassium hydroxide produced 2 ions, had a molar mass of 56.11 g/mol, and had a $\Delta H°_{diss}$ of −57.6 kJ/mol. Magnesium sulfate produced 2 ions, had a molar mass of 120.38 g/mol, and had a $\Delta H°_{diss}$ of −91.0 kJ/mol. Use POE. Student 1 writes, *The solution containing Salt B had a higher boiling point because Salt B produces more ions in solution than Salt A.* These findings do not agree with Table 1 for the given substances, which produced the same number of ions. Eliminate choice (C). Student 2 writes, *The solution containing Salt B had a higher boiling point because it had a lower molar mass (the mass of 6.02×10^{23} particles).* "Salt B" in this question is magnesium sulfate, which does not have a lower molar mass than potassium hydroxide, so you can eliminate choices (A) and (D). This leaves only choice (B), and the findings in the table do agree with Student 3's hypothesis.

24. **G** The passage gives the following information: The boiling temperature for the solution of Salt A was measured to be 104°C. The procedure was repeated with Salt B, which resulted in a boiling temperature of 110°C. According to this question, ammonium nitrate has a boiling point of 107°C, right between Salts A and B. According to Student 2, the solution containing Salt B had a higher boiling point because it had a lower molar mass. Therefore, because ammonium nitrate has a higher boiling point than Salt A, it must have a lower molar mass. Only choice (G) can work. Choices (H) and (J) can be eliminated because Student 2 does not discuss enthalpy change.

25. **A** According to Student 2, *the salt with the lower molar mass will result in more particles.* In other words, the lower the molar mass of a substance the more particles it will produce. According to Table 1, sodium chloride has a molar mass of 58.4 g/mol, potassium hydroxide has a molar mass of 56.11 g/mol, and magnesium sulfate has a molar mass of 120.38 g/mol. Since potassium hydroxide has the lowest molar mass, it should produce the *most* particles. With this information alone, you can eliminate choices (B), (C), and (D). Only choice (A) remains and puts the substances in the correct relation to one another.

26. **F** The passage states, the mixture was heated and temperature readings acquired every 30 sec until the solution reached a full boil and the solid had completely dissolved. Since the mixture is only heated, it can be inferred that its temperature increases only. There's no indication that the substance is ever cooled, so choice (F) is the only answer supported by information from the passage.

27. **D** Student 3 offers the following hypothesis: The solution containing the salt with the more negative $\Delta H°_{diss}$ value will release more heat and thus result in a greater boiling point. According to Table 1, magnesium sulfate has the most negative $\Delta H°_{diss}$ value at −91.0 kJ/mol. Therefore, according to student 3, this substance should have the greatest boiling point of the substances listed.

28. H   Compare the new values given in the question to those for calcium chloride given in Table 1. Cesium hydroxide produces 2 ions, where calcium chloride produces 3. Student 1 writes, *The solution containing Salt B had a higher boiling point because Salt B produces more ions in solution than Salt A.* According to this hypothesis, calcium chloride produces more ions, so it should have a higher boiling point. The findings therefore support the hypothesis of Student 1, eliminating choices (G) and (J). Cesium hydroxide has a molar mass 149.91 g/mol, where calcium chloride has a molar mass of 111.0 g/mol. Student 2 writes, *The solution containing Salt B had a higher boiling point because it had a lower molar mass (the mass of 6.02×10^{23} particles).* According to this hypothesis, calcium chloride has a lower molar mass, so it should have a higher boiling point. The findings therefore support the hypothesis of Student 2, eliminating choice (F). There's no need to test the findings against Student 3's hypothesis: The only option left is choice (H).

29. C   According to Student 2, the salt with the lower molar mass will result in more particles and a greater solution boiling point than a salt with a greater molar mass. Student 2 is not concerned with "enthalpy change," so you can eliminate choices (B) and (D) immediately. According to Table 1, sodium chloride has a molar mass of 58.4 g/mol and ammonium nitrate has a molar mass of 80.1 g/mol. Therefore, because sodium chloride has a smaller molar mass it should have a greater boiling point, as suggested in choice (C).

Passage VI

30. G   According to Figure 3, the marine deposition of Mg^{2+} is highest in February and lowest in November, making choice (G) the correct answer. The marine deposition of Cl^- is highest in June and lowest in October, eliminating choice (F). The marine deposition of Na^+ is highest in November and lowest in July, eliminating choice (H). The marine deposition of SO_4^{2-} is highest in January and lowest in October, eliminating choice (J).

31. B   Look carefully at Figure 2. The marine deposition of Cl^- is around 950 kg/m^3 except in June, at which point it is much higher. Because it has only this single outlier, we can reasonably expect that the *mean*, or *average*, monthly deposition will be closer to 950, as choice (B) suggests.

32. H   This question is difficult to answer "Yes" or "No" immediately, so work with the reasons given in each of the answer choices. Use Figure 3 to check these reasons. According to Figure 3, the monthly deposition of Na^+ is highest in the winter months and lowest in the summer months. We can therefore eliminate choices (G) and (J), which give information that contradicts Figure 3. This information then *supports* the statement in the problem that the *marine deposition of Na$^+$ is highest in the winter and lowest in the summer*, thus making choice (H) the correct answer.

33. A   The introduction to the passage gives the following information: *Ions in seawater, such as Cl$^-$, SO$_4^{2-}$, Na$^+$, and Mg$_2^+$, are carried down ocean floor through a process known as* marine deposition. Therefore, in order for there to be *marine deposition*, ions must be *carried down* somewhere. If the water does not move during an entire month, then the ions will not move and no marine deposition will occur doing this month.

34. J   Make sure you pay careful attention to the key in Figure 4. According to Figure 4, the annual marine depositions of both ions were lower in the Arctic Ocean, the site farthest from the Atlantic Ocean. The annual marine depositions of both ions increase as the sensor gets closer to the Atlantic Ocean site.

35. D   According to Figure 3, the marine deposition of SO_4^{2-} was not studied, eliminating choice (A). The marine deposition of Mg^{2+} changed during the study, eliminate choice (B). According to Figure 1, the movement of water during the month changed every month during the twelve-month period, eliminating choice (C). Only the location of the study, the Atlantic Ocean, was held constant, making choice (D) the correct answer. The location of the study was not changed until Study 3.

Passage VII

36. F   Use Figure 1. The key in the corner of the graph says that the anything graphed with a solid line is *blue* and anything graphed with a dotted line is *colorless*. The curve shown in this graph changes from solid to dotted at 1 mL of titrite added, meaning that all the solution at all values less than 1 mL will be blue and the solution at all values greater than 1 mL will be colorless. The only one of the answer choices that gives a value less than 1 mL is choice (F).

37. D   The blurb contains the following sentence: Starch and I_2 form a complex with a deep blue color, but when I_2 is reduced to 2 iodide (I^-) ions, the complex dissipates and the solution becomes colorless. In other words, when the solution is reduced, it becomes colorless. According to Figure 2, the solution is colorless (and therefore reduced) above 1 mL of titrite added. Only choice (D) gives a value greater than 1 mL.

38. J   Figure 2 does not show the voltage at 2.5 mL of titrite added, but the curve follows a clear trend. As the volume of titrant added increases, the voltage increases as well. At 2 mL of titrite added, the voltage is equivalent to 7 kV. Therefore, at 2.5 mL of titrant added, the voltage will most likely be greater than 7 kV, as in choice (J).

39. C   The experiment detailed in this passage is described in the first line as follows: Oxidation-reduction titration is a method in which precise volumes of a titrant (an oxidizing or reducing agent) are added dropwise to a known volume of an analyte (a reducing or oxidizing agent, respectively). In other words, one substance (the titrant) is added gradually to a certain amount of another substance (the analyte). Therefore, when Experiment 1 says that the I_2 solution was incrementally added to the SO_2 solution, it can be inferred that the I_2 is the titrant and the SO_2 is the analyte. In Experiment 2, the sodium thiosulfate solution was used instead of the SO_2 solution; therefore, in Experiment 2, the I_2 is still the titrant, and the sodium thiosulfate solution is the analyte, as in choice (C). If you picked choice (D), be careful—you may not have noticed the change from Experiment 1 to Experiment 2.

40. G   Use POE. Experiment 1 contains the following information: *A potentiometer, which acts as a control input for electronic circuits, was placed in the solution.* The key word here is *electric currents.* There's nothing to suggest that the potentiometer has anything to do with *concentration,* eliminating choice (F), or *freezing* or *boiling point,* eliminating choices (H) and (J). Only choice (G) contains any reference to *electric currents* and is therefore the best answer.

41. C   Use POE. If you're not sure how to answer "Yes" or "No," have a look at the reasons. According to the blurb, starch and I_2 form a complex with a deep blue color, but when I_2 is reduced to 2 iodide (I^-) ions, the complex dissipates and the solution becomes colorless. In other words, when the solution is reduced, it becomes colorless. At 0.2 mL of titrant added, the solution is blue, and at 1.8 mL of titrant added, the solution is colorless. Eliminate choices (B) and (D), whose reasons contradict this information. Then, answer the question: Do these findings agree with the scientist's hypothesis? They don't, because the titrant is not reduced at values below 1 mL, so the answer must be "No," eliminating choice (A). Only choice (C) remains.

Math Introduction

In some ways, the Math test of the ACT is the content-heaviest of all the tests: In other words, there are many problems on the Math that test concepts similar to those you've learned in your Math classes. In fact, ACT makes a big deal about how "curricular" the exam is, claiming that the Math test is "designed to assess the mathematical skills students have typically acquired in courses taken up to the beginning of grade 12." They even go so far as to offer a list of how the topics will break down in any given administration.

Topic	Number of Questions
Pre-algebra	14
Elementary Algebra	10
Intermediate Algebra	9
Plane Geometry	14
Coordinate Geometry	9
Trigonometry	4

But as with all things ACT, these distinctions may not mean a ton to you, the test-taker. Nor should they. At best, this chart should help to drive home one main point:

> The Math test of the ACT is roughly half Algebra and half Geometry.

While there's really no substitute for a solid and complete knowledge of Math fundamentals (and not-so-fundamentals), there are a number of ways you can still get a really great Math score by being a smart test-taker. You've already seen in the Introduction to this book (pages 4–5) some of the pacing strategies that can help you maximize your scores.

The ACT Math test is in Order of Difficulty. Keep an eye on the question numbers!

Let's have a look in the next two chapters at some of the specific ways you can improve your scores in Algebra and Geometry. As we move through the two chapters in this book, keep an eye on the problem number. ACT Math is the one section that is in Order of Difficulty, so the problem numbers offer a nice gauge of how difficult ACT considers certain concepts and types of Word Problems.

Algebra

So you've got roughly 33 algebra questions to tackle on any given Math test. It's probably a good idea to comb the test looking for those 14 pre-algebra questions first, and then to track down the 10 elementary-algebra questions, and then to go back and look for the intermediate-algebra questions, right? No way! That would be a tremendous waste of time, and even a nearly impossible task—what are the distinctions among these three categories anyway?

For our money, it's best to think of Algebra problems (and really all Math problems) as broken down into two categories: *Plug-and-Chug* and *Word Problems*. Many of the Math skills you use in these problems will be the same, but each will require a slightly different approach, for the obvious reason that Word Problems require that you deal with, well, words.

But let's start with a nice, straightforward, "Plug and Chug" problem:

MADSPM
(Multiply/Add, Divide/Subtract, Power/Multiply)

When you *multiply* two bases, you *add* their exponents.

$$\text{e.g., } x^2 \times x^3 = x^5$$

When you *divide* two bases, you *subtract* their exponents.

$$\text{e.g., } \frac{x^5}{x^3} = x^2$$

When you raise a base to a *power*, you *multiply* the exponents.

$$\text{e.g, } \left(x^2\right)^3 = x^6$$

25. The expression $-4y^2\left(9y^7 - 3y^5\right)$ is equivalent to:

   A. $-36y^9 + 12y^7$

   B. $-36y^9 - 12y^7$

   C. $-36y^{14} + 12y^{10}$

   D. $-36y^{14} - 12y^{10}$

   E. $-24y^4$

Here's How To Crack It
Sure, there are words in this problem, but all it's really asking you to do is to match up the expression in the question with one of the expressions in the answer choices. Remember to distribute and use MADSPM.

Let's see how this works with the equation given in question 25.

$$-4y^2(9y^7 - 3y^5) = y^2(-36y^7 + 12y^5)$$
$$= -36y^9 + 12y^7$$

This matches up with choice (A). If you worked through this problem and got one of the other answer choices, think about what you may have done wrong. If you chose (B), you may have forgotten to distribute the negative sign when you multiplied the −4. If you chose (C), you may have multiplied the exponents rather than adding them together. If you chose (D), you may have multiplied the exponents and forgotten to distribute the negative. If you chose (E), you may have forgotten that you can only add and subtract exponents when the bases are the same.

Whatever the case may be, don't sell these problems short. Even though they don't take as long, they're worth just as much as the "harder" problems. Recall from the introduction how few questions you really need to pull up your math score. Make sure you work carefully on all your Now and Later questions. There is no partial credit on the ACT, so a careless error leaves you with an answer just as wrong as a random guess.

> Fixing a few careless math errors can improve your ACT Math score significantly by ensuring that you get all the points on questions you know how to do.

Let's have a look at another.

43. $4x^2 + 20x + 24$ is equivalent to:

    A. $(4x+4)(x+6)$
    B. $(4x-4)(x-6)$
    C. $(4x+24)(x-1)$
    D. $2(2x-4)(x-3)$
    E. $2(2x+4)(x+3)$

This one looks a lot like the last one, but the math is a good deal more difficult. In fact, even if you're pretty good at factoring quadratic equations, you might still find this one to be a bit of an issue. If you can do the factoring quickly and accurately, great, but if not, help is on the way!

PLUGGING IN

When you look at the topic breakdown for the ACT, what is it about "Pre-algebra" that sounds so much easier than "Intermediate" or even "Elementary Algebra"? Well, for one thing, with Algebra inevitably come *variables*. You probably remember first hearing about these things in sixth or seventh grade and thinking to yourself how much easier life was when math was just plain numbers.

Here's the good news. Many of the algebra problems on the ACT, even the most complex, can be solved with what we like to call *Plugging In*. What Plugging In enables you to do is to solve difficult variable problems using basic arithmetic.

First, you'll need to identify whether you can Plug In.

Plug In when:

there are variables in the answer choices.

there are variables in the question.

the question is dealing with fractions, percents, or other relational numbers.

Here's How to Crack It

Plugging In works with both Word Problems and Plug and Chug questions. Question 43 may look like it requires a "content-based" approach, but let's see how much easier it is if we Plug In.

First, let's Plug In a number for the variable. The best numbers to Plug In are usually small and easy to deal with: numbers like 2, 5, and 10. Let's try 2 in this problem. If $x = 2$,

$$4(2)^2 + 20(2) + 24 = 4(4) + 20(2) + 24$$
$$= 16 + 40 + 24$$
$$= 56 + 24$$
$$= 80$$

So if we Plug In 2 everywhere there's an x, the expression gives us 80. Now, since the question is merely asking for an equivalent expression, we will want the same result as we plug our value into the answer choices. In this case, 80 is our *target answer*. Let's go to the answer choices and see which one matches up:

43. $4(2)^2 + 20(2) + 24$ is equivalent to $\boxed{80}$.
   A. $(4(2) + 4)((2) + 6) = (12)(8) = 96$
   B. $(4(2) - 4)((2) - 6) = (4)(-4) = -16$
   C. $(4(2) - 24)((2) - 1) = (-16)(1) = -16$
   D. $2(2(2) - 4)((2) - 3) = 2(0)(-1) = 0$
   E. $2(2(2) + 4)((2) + 3) = 2(8)(5) = 80$

The only one that matches up is choice (E), the correct answer. No quadratic formula or difficult factoring required!

Let's review the steps:

> Once you've determined that you can Plug In, follow these steps.
>
> 1. Plug In an easy-to-use value for your variable or variables.
>
> 2. Work the information in the question using the numbers you've Plugged In to find a *target answer.*
>
> 3. Plug the variables into the answer choices to find the one that matches up with the target.
>
> 4. Make sure you check all the answer choices. If more than one answer choice works, plug in a new set of numbers and try again.

Let's try another one.

---

28. As part of an analysis to determine how summer vacations affect students' retention of school materials, scientists conducted an experiment. As shown in the chart below, they showed the time, d days, since the student had finished and the number of facts, f, that the student remembered from the previous year.

d	1	3	5	7	9
f	96	72	48	24	0

Which of the following equations represents all the data found in this study?

   F. $f = 9 - d$

   G. $f = 3(9 - d)$

   H. $f = 3d + 3$

   J. $f = 3(36 - 4d)$

   K. $f = 96d$

Here's How to Crack It

This problem looks very different from our last two, but notice that it has some important features in common with them. Most important for our purposes are the variables in the answer choices. With these we know that we can Plug In on this question.

This problem is much bulkier than the last two, though, and in many ways more intimidating. This is because it's a *Word Problem*. As we mentioned earlier in this chapter, even though Word Problems often use the same mathematical concepts, they ask about them in much more convoluted ways. Here's a simple Basic Approach for dealing with Word Problems.

When dealing with Word Problems on the ACT Math test:

1. **Know the question**. Read the whole problem before calculating anything, and underline the actual question.

2. **Let the answers help**. Look for clues on how to solve and ways to use POE (Process of Elimination).

3. **Break the problem into bite-sized pieces**. Watch out for tricky phrasing.

Let's use these steps to solve this problem.

1. **Know the question.** We need to find an equation that can accommodate all of the information in the table for d and f. The question in this problem is below the chart. How much of the other stuff do we need? Not much.

2. **Let the answers help.** Remember how important the answers have been in what we've done so far in this chapter. If there are variables in those answer choices, we can usually Plug In. We have variables in these answer choices, so we'll plan to Plug In here.

3. **Break the problem into bite-sized pieces.** We know we need an equation that will work for all the points in this chart. Let's pick one set of points that will be easy to test, and then a second set to confirm our answers. Go easy on yourself! There's no reason to pick the biggest numbers. Let's try first the point to the far right of the chart: $d = 9$, $f = 0$. We want an equation that will work for these points, so let's try the answers:

F.	$0 = 9 - 9$	✓
G.	$0 = 3(9 - 9)$	✓
H.	$0 = 3(9) + 3$	✗
J.	$0 = 3(36 - 4(9))$	✓
K.	$0 = 96(9)$	✗

Okay, we've eliminated two of the answer choices. Now let's try another set of points: $d = 7, f = 24$.

    F. $24 = 9 - 7$ ✗

    G. $24 = 3(9 - 7)$ ✗

    H. $f = 3d + 3$

    J. $24 = 3(36 - 4(7))$ ✓

    K. $f = 96d$

Only one remains, and our best answer is (J). All using basic arithmetic in the formulas provided.

———————————◯———————————

PLUGGING IN THE ANSWERS

Now, what happens when we don't have the hallmarks of easy Plugging In problems: variables in the answer choices or in the problem? Like question 45:

———————————◯———————————

45. A high-school basketball player has shot 170 free throws and has made 100 of those free throws. Starting now, if she makes each free throw she attempts, what is the least number of free throws she must attempt in order to raise her free-throw percentage to at least 70% ?

    A. 19

    B. 20

    C. 63

    D. 64

    E. 70

In this problem, there are no variables anywhere to be seen. Still, we're going to need to put together some kind of equation or something that will enable us to answer the question. For this one, we can *Plug in the Answers* (PITA).

PITA when:

    the question asks for a specific amount. Look for "How many?" or "How much?" or "What is the value of?"

    there are no variables in the answer choices.

Question 45 is a Word Problem, so let's go through the steps:

1. **Know the question.** We need to figure out how many additional free throws this player will need to have a free-throw percentage of 70%. Also, when ACT italicizes or capitalizes a word, pay special attention. In this case, they've italicized the word *least*. Keep this in mind, it tells you that a number of the answer choices may work, but the correct will be the *least* of these. The phrase "What is the least number?" is the kind of very specific question that usually makes for a good PITA problem.
2. **Let the answers help.** There are no variables in these answer choices, and that coupled with the fact that it asks for a specific value is a good indication that we'll be using these answer choices to PITA. Notice the answer choices are listed in ascending order, which means it might be smart to start with the middle choice. That way we can eliminate answers that are too high or too low.
3. **Break the problem into bite-sized pieces.** With many PITA problems, it can help to create columns building on the information given in the answer choices and the problem. Start with the question that's being asked: You've already got five possible answers to that question.

45. A high-school basketball player has shot 170 free throws and has made 100 of those free throws. Starting now, if she makes each free throw she attempts, <u>what is the least number of free throws she must attempt in order to raise her free-throw percentage to at least 70% ?</u>

Free-throws	Total free-throws	Total completed	Percentage free-throws
A. 19			
B. 20			
C. 63	233	163	69.9%
D. 64			
E. 70			

Here's How To Crack It
As choice (C) has shown, 63 additional free throws only raises the percentage to 69.9%. We know this is wrong because we want to raise it to 70%. Therefore, since choice (C) gives a value that is too small, choices (A) and (B) must be too small as well. Let's try choice (D).

Our best answer here is choice (D), because it produces a free-throw percentage of 70.1%. Choice (E) will produce a percentage greater than 70% as well, but remember, this question is asking for the *least*.

45. A high-school basketball player has shot 170 free throws and has made 100 of those free throws. Starting now, if she makes each free throw she attempts, <u>what is the least number of free throws she must attempt in order to raise her free-throw percentage to at least 70% ?</u>

Free-throws	Total free-throws	Total completed	Percentage free-throws
A. 19	189	89	47.1
B. 20	190	90	47.4%
C. 63	233	163	69.9%
D. 64	234	164	70.1%
E. 70			

Let's review what we've learned about this type of question so far.

When you've identified a problem as a PITA problem:

Start with the middle answer choice. This can help with POE (process of elimination).

Label your answer choices—they answer the question you underlined in the problem.

When you find the correct answer, stop! But make sure you're answering the right question.

Make sure you account for all the relevant information. PITA is most effective in simplifying difficult Word Problems, but make sure you've got everything you need!

Let's try another problem.

18. The product of two distinct integers is 192. If the sum of those same two integers is 28, what is the value of the larger of the two integers?

F. 18
G. 16
H. 12
J. 10
K.   8

Here's How to Crack It

Let's go through the steps.

1. Know the question. "What is the value of the larger of the two integers?" The key word here is *larger*. The numbers in the answer choices will be possibilities for this *larger* value. Notice this is asking for a specific value, which means we can PITA.
2. Let the answers help. We've got a list of non-variable answers in ascending order. Each one offers a possible answer to the specific question posed in the problem. Let's PITA, and use the answers to work backwards through the problem.
3. Break the problem into bite-sized pieces. Even though this is a short problem, there's a lot of information here, so we should use columns to help us keep all the information straight. The problem says that the *sum* of the two integers is 28, so let's start there. Begin with answer choice (C) to help with Process of Elimination.

18. The product of two distinct integers is 192. If the sum of those same two integers is 28, <u>what is the value of the larger of the two integers?</u>

Larger integer	Smaller integer	(Larger × Smaller) = 192?
F. 18		
G. 16		
H. 12	16	CAN'T WORK
J. 10		
K. 8		

We can eliminate choice (H) right off the bat. Just from what we've found, 12 can't be the *larger* integer if 16 is the *smaller* integer. We will therefore need a number larger than 12, so we can eliminate choices (J) and (K) as well. Let's try choice (G).

18. The product of two distinct integers is 192. If the sum of those same two integers is 28, <u>what is the value of the larger of the two integers?</u>

Larger integer	Smaller integer	(Larger × Smaller) = 192?
F. 18		
G. 16	12	16 × 12 = 192 Yes!
~~H. 12~~	~~16~~	~~CAN'T WORK~~
~~J. 10~~		
~~K. 8~~		

Choice (G) works, so we can stop there. Notice how PITA and Plugging In have enabled us to do these problems quickly and accurately without getting bogged down in generating difficult algebraic formulas.

A NOTE ON PLUGGING IN AND PITA

Plugging In and PITA are not the only ways to solve these problems, and it may feel weird using these methods instead of trying to do these problems "the real way." You may have even found that you knew how to work with the variables in Plugging In problems or how to write the appropriate equations for the PITA problems. If you can do either of those things, you're already on your way to a great Math score.

But think about it this way. We've already said that ACT doesn't give any partial credit. So do you think doing it "the real way" gets you any extra points? It doesn't: On the ACT, a right answer is a right answer, no matter how you get it. "The real way" is great, but unfortunately, it's often a lot more complex and offers a lot more opportunities to make careless errors.

The biggest problem with doing things the real way, though, is that it essentially requires that you invent a new approach for every problem. Instead, notice what we've given you here: two strategies that will work toward getting you the right answer on any number of questions. You may have heard the saying, "Give a man a fish and you've fed him for a day, but teach a man to fish and you've fed him for a lifetime." Now, don't worry, our delusions of grandeur are not quite so extreme, but Plugging In and PITA are useful in a similar way. Rather than giving you a detailed description of how to create formulas and work through them for these problems that won't themselves ever appear on an ACT again, we're giving you a strategy that will help you to work through any number of similar problems in future ACTs.

Try these strategies on your own in the drill that concludes this chapter.

PLUGGING IN DRILL

2. If $\dfrac{3n}{4} - 7 = 2$, then $n =$

F. -9

G. $-\dfrac{7}{3}$

H. $\dfrac{7}{3}$

J. 9

K. 12

3. If $f(a) = \dfrac{a^2 - 24}{a + 8}$, what is the value of $f(12)$?

A. 6

B. 8

C. 12

D. 20

E. 120

4. $-x^3 + 24x + 75 + 34x^3 - 36x$ is equivalent to:

F. $99x$

G. $-35x^3$

H. $24x + 75$

J. $33x^3 - 12x + 75$

K. $35x^3 + 12x + 75$

11. If b is a positive integer greater than 1, what is the smallest integer value of a for which there exists a value of b such that $\sqrt{a} - b^2 > 0$?

A. 5

B. 16

C. 25

D. 36

E. 49

13. Which of the following expressions is equivalent to $n^3 - n^2$?

A. $n^2(n + 1)$

B. $n(n - 1)$

C. $n^2(n - 1)$

D. n

E. $n(n^2 - 1)$

18. Amethyst's route to work is 48 miles long. Along the way, she stops for coffee and notices that the ratio of the number of miles she's driven so far to the number of miles left to go is 3:1. How many miles does she have left to drive?

F. 6

G. 12

H. 24

J. 30

K. 36

22. If $a + b = 42$ and $a - b = 16$, what is the value of b ?

F. 8

G. 13

H. 24

J. 29

H. 58

24. A salesman earns \$600 per week in base salary. For each successful sale, he receives \$125 in commission. Which of the following represents the amount of money, in dollars, the salesman earns in a given week in which he makes s successful sales?

F. $725s$

G. $125s - 600$

H. $600s + 125$

J. $600 - 125s$

K. $600 + 125s$

27. The expression $(n^2 - 6n + 5)(n + 4)$ is equivalent to:

A. $n^3 - 2n^2 - 19n + 20$

B. $n^3 - n^2 + 9n + 20$

C. $n^3 - 2n^2 - 7n + 20$

D. $n^3 + 2n^2 - 24n + 20$

E. $n^3 - 2n^2 - 29n + 20$

28. If $|n - 6| = 17$, what are the possible values of n ?

F. -23 and 11

G. -23 and 23

H. -11 and 23

J. -11 and 11

K. 28 only

31. If the area of a circle is 36π inches, what is the diameter of the circle, in inches?

A. 4
B. 6
C. 12
D. 18
E. 36

32. If $f(a) = a^2 + 3$ and $g(a) = 3a - 1$, which of the following is an expression for $g(f(a))$?

F. $a^2 + 3a + 2$
G. $3a^2 - 3$
H. $-a^2 + 3a - 2$
J. $3a^2 + 9a - 3$
K. $3a^2 + 8$

40. In a professional sports league consisting of x teams, y represents the number of teams that qualify for the playoffs in a given season. Which of the following could be used to determine the fraction of teams that does NOT make the playoffs in a given season?

F. $\dfrac{x - y}{x}$

G. $\dfrac{y - x}{x}$

H. $\dfrac{y}{x}$

J. $\dfrac{x - y}{y}$

K. $\dfrac{x + y}{x}$

41. If n is an integer, which of the following is a factor of the sum of $5n$ and $12n$?

A. 5
B. 12
C. 17
D. 34
E. 60

45. Which of the following gives the solution set for $\sqrt[3]{(n^2 - 6n)} = 3$?

A. {3}
B. {$2 \pm \sqrt{3}$ }
C. {−3, 9}
D. {3, −9}
E. {27}

46. If $x > y$, then $-|y - x|$ is equivalent to which of the following?

F. $\sqrt{y - x}$
G. $x - y$
H. $|y - x|$
J. $-(x - y)$
K. $|x - y|$

48. If x is a negative integer, which of the following must be a positive integer?

F. 0^x
G. x^0
H. $x + 4$
J. $-x^4$
K. x^x

49. If n is a real number, what is the solution of the equation $9^{1-n} = 3^{1+n}$?

A. $-\dfrac{2}{3}$

B. $-\dfrac{1}{3}$

C. $\dfrac{1}{3}$

D. $\dfrac{1}{2}$

E. $\dfrac{4}{3}$

55. Which of the following is an irrational value of n that is a solution to the equation $|n^2 - 30| - 6 = 0$?

A. $\sqrt{6}$
B. 6
C. $2\sqrt{6}$
D. $3\sqrt{6}$
E. $4\sqrt{6}$

59. Consider all pairs of positive integers a and b whose sum is 6. For how many values of a does $a^b = b^a$?

A. None
B. 1
C. 2
D. 3
E. 6

ANSWERS

2. K
3. A
4. J
11. C
13. C
18. G
22. G
24. K
27. A
28. H
31. C
32. K
40. F
41. C
45. C
46. J
48. G
49. C
55. C
59. D

EXPLANATIONS

2. **K** Plug In the Answers on this one. No harm in starting with the middle answer choice, but if you want this problem to be as easy as possible (and it is question 2, so it should be relatively easy), you might try the whole numbers in the answers first. With choice (J), it means that $\frac{3(9)}{4} - 2 = 7$. Since $\frac{3(9)}{4} = 6.75$, you can eliminate it. Try choice (K): $\frac{3(12)}{4} - 2 = 7$. $\frac{3(12)}{4} = 9$, and $9 - 2 = 7$, so you've found your answer.

3. **A** Here, ACT is telling you what to Plug In: When you see a function and you're given a number inside the parentheses, Plug In that number everywhere in the function that you see the variable. So, $f(12) = \frac{12^2 - 24}{12 + 8}$. That results in $\frac{120}{20}$, which means the answer is 6.

4. **J** While algebra works on this one, the safest bet is to Plug In. Since there are exponents, pick a small number, like 2. $-2^3 + 24(2) + 75 + 34(2)^3 - 36(2)$. This simplifies to $-8 + 48 + 75 + 272 - 72$. When you combine all those numbers, you get a target answer of 331. When you go to the answer choices, look for that same number. In choice (J), you have $33(2)^3 - 12(2) + 75$. Since $264 - 12 + 75 = 331$, you have your answer.

11. **C** This is a tricky and confusing problem made simple by Plugging In the Answers. Since the problem asks for the smallest possible value of a, start with the smallest answer choice. Work your way up to 25, and the problem reads $\sqrt{25 - b^2} > 0$. The question becomes, "Is there a value of b (remember, b must be an integer greater than 1) that makes that equation true?" Sure there is: If $b = 2$, then $5 - 4 > 0$.

13. **C** Plug In your own number since you see variables in the answers. If $x = 3$, then the expression is $3^3 - 3^2 = 27 - 9$; your target answer is 18. Plugging in $x = 3$, the only answer choice that matches the target is choice (C): $3^2(3-1) = 9(2) = 18$.

18. **G** Note that the problem is asking for the number of miles left to go. Plug In the Answers starting with choice (H). If she has 24 miles left, then she's halfway there—that's not far enough along, so eliminate choice (H) and any answer with higher mileage. Plug in choice (G). If she's got 12 miles left to go, that means $48 - 12 = 36$, meaning she's driven 36 miles so far. Since the ratio of 36:12 is 3:1, this is your answer.

22. **G** Plug In the Answers starting with choice (H). You'll know you've found the answer when you get the same value for a in both equations. This works with choice (G): If $a + 13 = 42$, then $a = 29$, and if $a - 13 = 16$, then $a = 29$.

24. K   Plug In a small number for the number of sales he's completed so the math is as easy as possible. If he completed 2 sales, then he's made $250 commission to go with his $600 base salary, for total earnings of $850. Choice (K) gets you the same value.

27. A   Play it safe and Plug In 2. $(2^2 - 6(2) + 5)(2 + 4)$ means $(4 - 12 + 5)(6)$, which gives you -18 as a target answer. Choice (A) will read $2^3 - 2(2)^2 - 19(2) + 20$. Simplified, $8 - 8 - 38 + 20 = -18$.

28. H   When the absolute value of an expression is equal to a number, you can set up two separate equations, one equal to the positive value and one equal to its negative equivalent. In this case, $n - 6 = 17$ and $n - 6 = -17$. Plug In each pair of numbers in the answer choices. In choice (H), $23 - 6 = 17$ and $-11 - 6 = -17$.

31. C   Plug in the circle's area into the area formula: $r^2 = 36$ to determine the radius is 6. The question asks for the diameter, which is twice the radius, so the answer is choice (C). Be careful not to pick choice (B), which is a partial answer.

32. K   When you have one function inside another, start with the one on the inside and work your way out. And of course…Plug In! So Plug In 2, and start with $f(2) = 2^2 + 3$. That means $f(2) = 7$. That's now the value you can Plug In to the other function. $g(7) = 3(7) - 1$, so your target answer is 20. Plug 2 into the answer choices, and choice (K) will read $3(2)^2 + 8$, which is 20.

40. F   Plug In values for the number of teams in the league and the number of teams that qualify for the playoffs. Say there are 15 teams in the league (represented by x) and 8 of them qualify (represented by y). That leaves 7 for the number of teams that do not qualify, which means that your target answer is $\frac{7}{15}$. Choice (F) becomes $\frac{15-8}{15}$, or $\frac{7}{15}$.

41. C   Here, you may need to Plug In multiple times. Make $n = 2$, and the sum of 12(2) and 5(2) is 34. Both choices (C) and (D) work. But make $n = 1$, and the sum of 12(1) and 5(1) is 17, eliminating choice (D).

45. C   To make things a little easier, you can cube both sides to get rid of the radical. The right side of the equation is now 27. Now, Plug In the Answers and see which one works. In choice (C), $(-3)^2 - 6(-3) = 9 - (-18) = 27$, and $(9)^2 - 6(9) = 81 - 54 = 27$.

46. J   Plug In anything you want as long as $x > y$, such as $x = 3$ and $y = 2$. In the original problem, $-|2 - 3| = -|-1|$, so the target answer is -1. Try this out in the answer choices. Choice (J) works: $-(3 - 2) = -1$.

48. G   Plug In any negative integer for x and try each answer choice out. Since any number, positive or negative, raised to the power of 0 is 1, that's the only answer that works.

49. C   Plug In the Answers to avoid the confusing algebra with exponents. Starting with choice (C), use your calculator to determine whether the equation $9^{1\frac{1}{3}} = 3^{1+\frac{1}{3}}$.

55. C   The problem asks for an irrational solution, so while choice (B) would work, it is rational, so cross it off. Then Plug In the Answers. When you Plug In the value in choice (C), the equation reads $\left|(2\sqrt{6})^2 - 30\right| - 6 = 0$. When you square $2\sqrt{6}$, you get 24, so it's $\left|24 - 30\right| - 6 = 0$. The value inside the absolute value symbol becomes -6, the absolute value of which is 6. The final equation is now much simpler: $6 - 6 = 0$.

59. D   First, figure out all the pairs of positive integers which add up to 6 and Plug them In. 1^5 and 5^1 aren't equal, so try 2 and 4. $2^4 = 4^2$. Be sure to keep track of what the problem asks: how many values of a satisfy the equation. Consider that a could occupy the place of either the 2 or the 4, so those are 2 possible values for a. The last pair of numbers is 3 and 3. Since $3^3 = 3^3$, 3 is the third value for a.

Geometry

We've seen in the Algebra chapter that a smart test-taking strategy, in and of itself, can improve your Math score. That is no less true for Geometry problems, but for these you typically have to bring a bit more to the table. ACT doesn't give you the formulas like SAT does, so you need to have them stored in your brain (or your calculator) when test day rolls around. Remember, counting trigonometry, Geometry makes up about half of any given ACT Math test.

THE BASIC APPROACH
Let's try a straightforward geometry problem.

22. In right triangle $\triangle STU$ shown below, V is the midpoint of $\overline{TU}$. In inches, what is the length of $\overline{UV}$?

    F.   6
    G.   9
    H. 12
    J.   72
    K. 144

1. Ballpark
First, ACT has actually done us a big favor on this problem. While they claim that "illustrative figures are NOT necessarily drawn to scale," it's usually safe to assume that they are at least close. Remember what we're looking for here, the length of UV. Look closely at this figure: You can tell just by looking at it that the longest side is SU, which has a length of 13, so it's not likely that any smaller part of the triangle will have a longer length, eliminating choices (J) and (K). We can probably eliminate (H) as well, because SU is so much longer than UV. This way, if we were running short on time and had to guess, we have improved our chances of guessing from 20% to 50%. Not bad for no work, huh?

2. Write on the Figure
Now, let's dig in to get our final answer. Rather than trying to keep everything in your mind, make sure you are writing all over your figure. The problem says that V is the midpoint of $\overline{TU}$, so make sure you mark that on your figure. It's probably worth emphasizing the portion, $\overline{UV}$, that you are looking for as well.

3. Write Down Formulas

As for the formulas, get those down before you begin working the problem as well. For this problem, you are dealing with the sides of a right triangle, so it is likely that you will need the Pythagorean theorem: $a^2 + b^2 = c^2$, where c is the longest side. Plug in the information you have, and write anything new that you find on the figure:

$$a^2 + b^2 = c^2$$
$$(5)^2 + \left(\overline{TU}\right)^2 = (13)^2$$
$$\left(\overline{TU}\right)^2 = (13)^2 - (5)^2$$
$$= 169 - 25$$
$$= 144$$
$$\overline{TU} = 12$$

Don't make your brain work any harder than it needs to! Make sure you're writing everything down. Hopefully by now your scratch paper looks something like this:

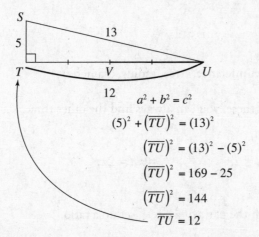

Now, once you've got all the information on the figure, it's probably very clear that the answer is choice (F), because $\overline{TU}$ is 12, and $\overline{UV}$ is one half of this value. If you know your Pythagorean triples, you may have found $\overline{TU}$ even more quickly, but make sure you're reading the question carefully. If you don't read all the way, you might fall into the trap and pick choice (H).

Pythagorean triples are easy-to-remember, commonly tested ratios for the sides of a right triangle. Memorizing them can save you a lot of time by enabling you to bypass the Pythagorean theorem. The most common Pythagorean triples are 3:4:5, 6:8:10, and 5:12:13, each listed from the shortest to the longest side. Which one does question 22 use?

So let's review the basic approach for Geometry problems.

> The Basic Approach on Geometry questions suggests:
>
> 1. Use ballparking to eliminate wrong answers on questions in which a figure is given.
>
> 2. Write any information given by the question on the provided figure.
>
> 3. Write down any formulas you need and Plug In any information you have.
>
> 4. If the question doesn't provide a figure, draw your own.

THE FORMULAS

Here are some of the formulas you may find useful on Geometry questions.

Circles

Think CArd! (Circumference, Area, radius, diameter)

If you have one of these, you can always find the other three.

$$d = 2r \qquad C = \pi d = 2\pi r \qquad A = \pi r^2$$

When dealing with the parts of a circle, set up a ratio.

$$\frac{part}{whole} = \frac{central\ angle}{360°} = \frac{arc}{2\pi r} = \frac{sector\ area}{\pi r^2}$$

For Coordinate Geometry, be able to recognize the equation of a circle:

$$(x - h)^2 + (y - k)^2 = r^2$$

where (h, k) is the center of the circle, and (x, y) is any point on the circle.

Triangles

$$\text{Area} = A = \frac{1}{2}bh$$

Perimeter: P = sum of the sides

Sum of all angles: 180°

Similar triangles have congruent angles and proportional sides.

Right Triangles

The Triangle rules apply, but there are some special rules for right triangles.

Pythagorean theorem, where a, b, and c are the sides of the triangle where c is the hypotenuse:

$$a^2 + b^2 = c^2$$

SOHCAHTOA (ratios between sides and angles of right triangles)

$$\sin \theta = \frac{\text{Opposite}}{\text{Hypotenuse}} \qquad \cos \theta = \frac{\text{Adjacent}}{\text{Hypotenuse}} \qquad \tan \theta = \frac{\text{Opposite}}{\text{Adjacent}}$$

Special Right Triangles

When you've determined the angles of your right triangle, use the following ratios to bypass the Pythagorean theorem:

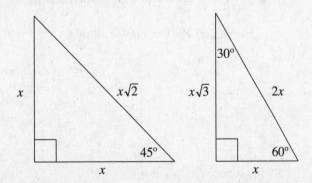

If a triangle problem contains a $\sqrt{2}$ or a $\sqrt{3}$, you can most likely use one of these special triangles.

If you don't know the angles, you can often bypass the Pythagorean theorem with the Pythagorean triples:

These Pythagorean triples are basic ratios, so they can be multiplied to be used with larger numbers.

6:8:10 is commonly cited as a Pythagorean triple, but it is just the 3:4:5 multiplied by 2.

Four-Sided Figures (Quadrilaterals)

Parallelogram: Opposite sides are parallel, opposite sides and angles are equal

Rhombus: Opposite sides parallel, ALL sides equal, opposite angles equal
    A rhombus is a *parallelogram* in which all four sides are equal.

Rectangle: Opposite sides parallel, opposite sides equal, ALL angles 90°
    A rectangle is a *parallelogram* with four right angles.

Square: Opposite sides parallel, ALL sides equal, ALL angles 90°
    A square is a type of *parallelogram*, *rhombus*, and *rectangle*.

For any of these four shapes:

Area: $A = bh$, where b and h are perpendicular

Perimeter: $P =$ the sum of all sides

Coordinate Geometry Formulas

All points are written (x,y) where x gives the x-coordinate and y gives the y-coordinate.

Two lines *intersect* when they meet at a single point.

$$\text{Slope: } \frac{rise}{run} = \frac{y_2 - y_1}{x_2 - x_1}$$

where (x_1, y_1) and (x_2, y_2) are two points on a line.

$$\text{Slope-intercept formula: } y = mx + b$$

where (x, y) is a point on the line, m is the slope, and b is the y-intercept, or the point at which the line crosses the y-axis.

Use the slope-intercept form when a question asks for the slope of a *perpendicular* line. The slope of a line perpendicular to it will be the opposite reciprocal or $-\frac{1}{m}$. That is, if slope of a line is 2, the slope of a perpendicular will be $-\frac{1}{2}$.

Parallel lines have equal slopes.

THE PROBLEMS

Plane Geometry

Let's use these formulas and the Basic Approach to solve some problems.

---

44. A circle has a diameter of 8 inches. What is the area of the circle, to the nearest 0.1 square inch?

   F. 12.6
   G. 25.1
   H. 50.3
   J. 64.0
   K. 201.1

Here's How To Crack It

Remember the Basic Approach. There's no figure, so draw your own. Once you've done that, mark it up with information from the problem, and get all your formulas down. Think CArd! Your paper should look something like this:

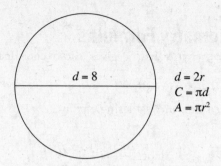

Now work the formulas to get the answer. We know that the diameter of this circle is 8, which means its radius is 4. Use the radius in the Area formula, and use your calculator to find this Area:

$$A = \pi r^2$$
$$A = \pi (4)^2$$
$$A = 16\pi$$
$$A \approx 50.3$$

This matches up nicely with choice (H). If you don't have a calculator, or you're not especially handy with it, no problem. Use ballparking. You know that π is roughly equivalent to 3, so your answer will need to be close to 16×3 or 48. Only choice (H) is close enough.

Coordinate Geometry

Let's try a Coordinate Geometry problem. ACT likes to make a big deal about the distinction between Plane and Coordinate Geometry, but as we'll see, your approach won't really differ at all.

23. In the standard (x,y) coordinate plane, point G lies at $(-3,-4)$ and point H lies at $(2,5)$. What is the length of $\overline{GH}$ in coordinate units?

A. 7

B. 4

C. $\sqrt{14}$

D. $\sqrt{45}$

E. $\sqrt{106}$

Here's How To Crack It

Your first impulse here will probably be to whip out the distance formula and complete this problem in lightning-fast time. The only problem is that the distance formula looks like this:

$$d = \sqrt{(x_2 - x_1)^2 + (y_2 - y_1)^2}$$

Yikes. If you've got this formula stored away in the RAM of your brain, great. Unfortunately, for most of us, this is a really easy formula to forget, or worse, to remember incorrectly. What you'll find about ACT Geometry is that for 90% of the problems, you're best off just dealing with the basics. For weird shapes in Plane Geometry, this will mean carving things up into recognizable shapes and working from there. On Coordinate Geometry, you will find that simple formulas and the Basic Approach can get you plenty of points.

Let's use the Basic Approach. First and foremost, this is a Geometry problem, and they haven't given you a figure. Draw your own. It should look something like this:

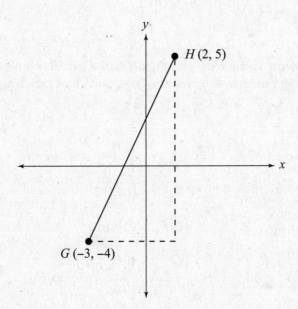

Now, look carefully at the line you've drawn for $\overline{GH}$. Remind you of anything? How about the hypotenuse of a right triangle? Remember, you want to work with the basics, and you know your triangles, so let's turn this thing into a right triangle.

Draw in the sides and find the lengths of those sides. To find the base of the triangle, figure out how much you're moving from one x-coordinate to the other. The points are $(-3, -4)$ and $(2, 5)$, so the x-coordinate will go from -3 to 2, or 5 units. The y-coordinate will go from -4 to 5, or 9 units. After you've drawn all this in and marked up your figure, you should have something like this:

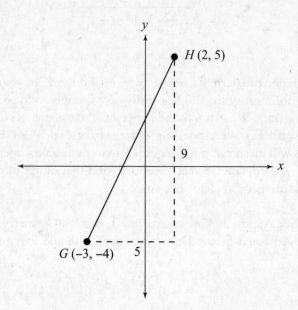

And now this is just a plain old ("plane" old?) Plane Geometry problem. You know two sides of a right triangle and need the third. Sounds like a job for the Pythagorean theorem.

$$a^2 + b^2 = c^2$$
$$(5)^2 + (9)^2 = \left(\overline{GH}\right)^2$$
$$\left(\overline{GH}\right)^2 = 25 + 81$$
$$\left(\overline{GH}\right)^2 = 106$$
$$\overline{GH} = \sqrt{106}$$

The answer is choice (E). And no distance formula required.

Trigonometry

There's a common misconception about the ACT regarding trigonometry. Many believe that if you don't have a solid foundation in trigonometry, you can't get a good score on the ACT Math Test. However, let's think back to the chart from the beginning of this lesson. Remember, there are only 4 trig questions on any given ACT.

What's more, two of these questions will deal with basic SOHCAHTOA, which you clearly don't need a whole semester or year of trig to learn. The other two questions may deal with radians, or the unit circle, or some of the trig identities, but you shouldn't worry about these until you've solidified a math score of at least 28.

So let's have a look at one of these basic SOHCAHTOA questions.

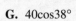

42. According to the measurements given in the figure below, which of the following expressions gives the distance, in meters, from the house to the garage?

F. $40\tan38°$

G. $40\cos38°$

H. $40\sin38°$

J. $\dfrac{40}{\cos38°}$

K. $\dfrac{40}{\sin38°}$

Here's How To Crack It

They've already written most of the information you'll need on the figure, but it can be worth noting the side that you are looking for: the side that shows the distance from the house to the garage.

Let the answer choices help. These choices tell you a lot more than you may think: First of all, they offer the main indication that this will be a SOHCAHTOA problem by showing that you will need to choose sine, cosine, or tangent. Next, they tell you that you'll only be dealing with one angle, the 38° one. Finally, they tell you that you won't need to do any weird rounding with decimals because they just want the sine, cosine, or tangent expression.

Have a close look at the sides you're dealing with. Where are they relative to the 38° angle? The base of the triangle is touching the 38° angle, so it's *adjacent*, and

Don't worry about Advanced Trigonometry concepts unless you are consistently scoring a 28 or higher on the ACT Math Test. It's way too much to learn for only two questions!

the side you're looking for is *opposite* the 38° angle. It looks like we won't be dealing with the *hypotenuse* at all. So which trig function deals with the *opposite* and *adjacent* sides? Remember SOHCAH**TOA**. The function we'll need is tangent. And don't do more work than you need to. Only choice (F) offers an expression featuring the tangent function, so it must be the correct answer.

Shapes Within Shapes: What's the Link?

ACT's favorite way to ask hard Geometry questions is to put shapes within shapes. You know the drill: Some shape inscribed in some other shape, or two shapes share a common side. They've got all kinds of ways to ask these questions. But when you see a shape drawn within another shape, there's usually one question that will blow the question wide open: *What's the link between the two shapes?* Let's try a few.

1. A square inscribed in a circle

2. A triangle inscribed in a rectangle

3. A square overlapping with a circle

So, what's the link?

1. What's the link? The diagonal of the square is the diameter of the circle.

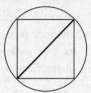

2. What's the link? The base of the triangle is the long side of the rectangle, and the height of the triangle is the short side of the rectangle.

3. What's the link? The side of the square is equivalent to the radius of the circle.

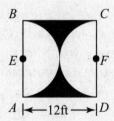

Let's try a problem that deals with these concepts.

37. In the square shown below, points E and F are the midpoints of sides $\overline{AB}$ and $\overline{CD}$, respectively. Two semicircles are drawn with centers E and F. What is the perimeter, in feet, of the shaded region?

A. $12 + 12\pi$
B. $24 + 12\pi$
C. $24 + 24\pi$
D. $48 + 12\pi$
E. $48 + 24\pi$

Here's How To Crack It

Make sure you write everything you need on the figure, including the relevant square and circle formulas. Since you are dealing with shapes within shapes, now is also a good time to figure out what the link is, what these two (or three, in this case) shapes have in common. Don't worry about digging up a formula for the perimeter of that hourglass-shaped thing. Stick with the shapes you know.

For this problem, the links occur on the right and left sides of the figure: The left and right sides of the square are the same as the diameters of each of the semi-circles. We can therefore say that if all sides of a square are equal, each of these sides is 12. Since the diameter of each semi-circle is equivalent to a side of the square, then the diameters of both semicircles must also be 12.

Let's use this information to find the perimeters of each of these semi-circles. Remember, when you're dealing with circles, the perimeter is called the *circumference*, which can be found with the formula $C = \pi d$. Since you're dealing with a semi-circle here, you'll need to divide its circumference in half. Let's find the circumference of the semicircle with center E.

$$\frac{C_E}{2} = \frac{\pi d}{2}$$
$$= \frac{\pi(12)}{2}$$
$$= 6\pi$$

The semicircle with center F will have the same circumference because it has the same diameter. Now all we need to do is add up our perimeters to find our answer. You know the sides of the square will each be 12 and the circumference of each semicircle will be 6π, so the total perimeter of the shaded region will be $12 + 12 + 6\pi + 6\pi = 24 + 12\pi$, choice (B).

So let's hear it once more:

> Don't do more work than you have to on Geometry problems by trying to remember every weird formula you've ever learned. Stick to the formulas you know, and work with the Basic Approach.

Now go ahead and give some of these concepts a try in the drill at the end of this chapter.

GEOMETRY DRILLS

Plane Geometry

6. In $\triangle XYZ$, $\angle X$ and $\angle Z$ are congruent, and the measure of $\angle Y$ is 122°. What is the measure of $\angle X$?

F. 29°
G. 60°
H. 61°
J. 58°
K. 122°

14. The 8-sided figure below is divided into 6 congruent squares. The total area of the 6 squares is 96 square centimeters. What is the perimeter, in centimeters, of the figure?

F. 16
G. 28
H. 48
J. 56
K. 96

20. The base of a triangle is 4 times the base of a smaller triangle. The 2 triangles have the same height. The area of the larger triangle is N square units. The area of the smaller triangle is xN square units. Which of the following is the value of x ?

F. $\dfrac{1}{16}$

G. $\dfrac{1}{8}$

H. $\dfrac{1}{4}$

J. 4

K. 16

24. What is the area, in square meters, of the figure below?

F. 40
G. 50
H. 108
J. 120
K. 144

27. In right triangle $\triangle FHK$ below, $\overline{GJ}$ is parallel to $\overline{FK}$, and $\overline{GJ}$ is perpendicular to $\overline{HK}$ at J. The length of $\overline{HK}$ is 12 inches, the length of $\overline{GJ}$ is 6 inches, and the length of $\overline{GH}$ is 10 inches. What is the length, in inches, of $\overline{FK}$?

A. 7
B. 8
C. 9
D. 10
E. 11

31. In the figure below, *JKLM* is a square. Points *N, O, P,* and *Q* are the midpoints of the sides of *JKLM*. Points *R, S, T,* and *V* are the midpoints of the sides of *NOPQ*. A side of *JKLM* is how many times as long as a side of *RSTV* ?

A. $\sqrt{2}$
B. 2
C. 3
D. 6
E. 8

37. The circle below has an area of 36π square meters. The circle is inscribed in the square and is tangent to the square at *W, X, Y,* and *Z*. What is the area, in square meters, of the square?

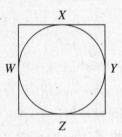

A. 6
B. 12
C. 18
D. 36
E. 144

48. In the figure below, the circle with center *X* has a radius of 8 centimeters and the measure of $\angle SRX$ is 70°. What is the measure of $\overset{\frown}{RS}$?

F. 20°
G. 40°
H. 50°
J. 55°
K. 70°

54. The side of an equilateral triangle is *s* inches longer than the side of a second equilateral triangle. How many inches longer is the altitude of the first triangle than the altitude of the second triangle?

F. $\dfrac{\sqrt{3}}{2}s$

G. $\sqrt{2}s$

H. $2s$

J. $3s$

K. s^3

55. In the figure below, the circles centers at *N* and *O* intersect at *X* and *Y*, and points *N, X, Y,* and *O* are collinear. The lengths of $\overline{MN}$, $\overline{OP}$, and $\overline{XY}$ are 10, 8, and 3 inches, respectively. What is the length, in inches, of $\overline{NO}$?

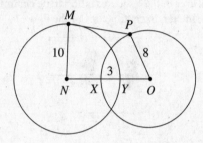

A. 10
B. 11
C. 12
D. 15
E. 18

Coordinate Geometry

3. A point at $(5, -4)$ in the standard (x,y) coordinate plane is shifted left 3 units and up 6 units. What are the new coordinates of the point?

   A. $(11, -7)$
   B. $(8, 2)$
   C. $(8, -10)$
   D. $(2, 2)$
   E. $(2, -10)$

13. The points $A(-6, 8)$ and $B(10, 2)$ lie in the standard (x,y) coordinate plane. What is the midpoint of $\overline{AB}$?

   A. $(-3, 4)$
   B. $(2, 5)$
   C. $(4, 10)$
   D. $(5, 1)$
   E. $(8, -3)$

17. What is the slope-intercept form of $5x - y + 2 = 0$?

   A. $y = -5x - 2$
   B. $y = -5x + 2$
   C. $y = 2x - 5$
   D. $y = 5x - 2$
   E. $y = 5x + 2$

24. Points $O(5, 3)$ and $P(-3, 8)$ lie in the standard (x,y) coordinate plane. What is the slope of $\overline{OP}$?

   F. $-\dfrac{5}{8}$

   G. $\dfrac{5}{8}$

   H. $-\dfrac{2}{11}$

   J. $\dfrac{2}{11}$

   K. $\dfrac{11}{2}$

33. What are the quadrants of the standard (x,y) coordinate plane below that contain points on the graph of the equation $8x + 4y = 12$?

quadrants of the standard
(x,y) coordinate plane

   A. II and IV only
   B. I, II, and III only
   C. I, II, and IV only
   D. I, III, and IV only
   E. II, III, and IV only

39. On a map in the standard (x,y) coordinate plane, the cities of Everton and Springfield are represented by the points $(-3, -5)$ and $(-6, -8)$, respectively. Each unit on the map represents an actual distance of 20 kilometers. Which of the following is closest to the distance, in kilometers, between these 2 cities?

   A. 316
   B. 120
   C. 85
   D. 60
   E. 49

41. Which of the following equations, when graphed in the standard (x,y) coordinate plane, would cross the x-axis at $x = -3$ and $x = 6$?

   A. $y = 3(x - 3)(x + 6)$
   B. $y = 3(x - 3)(x - 6)$
   C. $y = 3(x + 3)(x + 6)$
   D. $y = 6(x - 3)(x - 6)$
   E. $y = 6(x + 3)(x - 6)$

48. The graph of $f(x) = x^3$ is shown in the standard (x,y) coordinate plane below. For which of the following equations is the graph of the cubic function shifted 4 units to the left and 3 units up?

    F. $f(x) = (x-4)^3 - 3$
    G. $f(x) = (x-4)^3 + 3$
    H. $f(x) = (x+3)^3 - 4$
    J. $f(x) = (x+4)^3 + 3$
    K. $f(x) = (x+4)^3 - 3$

52. In the standard (x,y) coordinate plane, the graph of which of the following equations is a circle with center $(-3,5)$ and radius 4 coordinate units?

    F. $(x-3)^2 + (y+5)^2 = 4$
    G. $(x+3)^2 + (y-5)^2 = 4$
    H. $(x+3)^2 + (y+5)^2 = 16$
    J. $(x-3)^2 + (y+5)^2 = 16$
    K. $(x+3)^2 + (y-5)^2 = 16$

56. The graph below shows the distance a hot-air balloon is from the ground for a period of 10 minutes. A certain order of 3 of the following 5 actions describes the balloon's movement in relation to the position of the ground. Which order is it?

    I.   Remains stationary for 2 minutes
    II. Moves away at 3 yards per minute
    III. Moves toward at 3 yards per minute
    IV. Moves away at 1 yard per minute
    V. Moves toward at 1 yard per minute

    F. I, II, II
    G. II, I, V
    H. III, I, IV
    J. IV, I, III
    K. V, I, II

Trigonometry

21. In right triangle $\triangle LMN$ below, $\sin L = \dfrac{3}{8}$. Which of the following expressions is equal to $\sin M$?

A. $\dfrac{8}{3}$

B. $\dfrac{\sqrt{73}}{3}$

C. $\dfrac{\sqrt{55}}{3}$

D. $\dfrac{\sqrt{73}}{8}$

E. $\dfrac{\sqrt{55}}{8}$

22. The dimensions of the right triangle shown below are given in meters. What is $\tan \theta$?

F. $\dfrac{X}{Y}$

G. $\dfrac{X}{Z}$

H. $\dfrac{Y}{Z}$

J. $\dfrac{Y}{X}$

K. $\dfrac{Z}{X}$

24. The right triangle shown below has a height of 6 feet. The measure of the angle indicated is 8°. Which of the following is closest to the length, in feet, of the side opposite the 8° ?

(Note: $\sin 8° \approx 0.1392$ $\sin 82° \approx 0.9903$
$\cos 8° \approx 0.9903$ $\cos 82° \approx 0.1392$
$\tan 8° \approx 0.1405$ $\tan 82° \approx 7.1154)$

F. 0.141
G. 0.835
H. 0.843
J. 5.942
K. 42.692

29. For the polygon below, which of the following represents the length, in inches, of $\overline{FK}$?

A. 10

B. 30

C. $\dfrac{10}{\sin 70°}$

D. $\dfrac{30}{\sin 70°}$

E. $\sin 70°$

35. A right triangle is shown in the figure below. Which of the following expressions gives θ ?

1 m

0.25 m

θ

A. $\cos^{-1}\left(\dfrac{1}{4}\right)$

B. $\sin^{-1}\left(\dfrac{1}{4}\right)$

C. $\tan^{-1}\left(\dfrac{1}{4}\right)$

D. $\cos^{-1}(4)$

E. $\tan^{-1}(4)$

37. A person stands on level ground holding a kite string. The string 128 meters long is attached to the center of the kite and makes an angle of 64° with the ground, as shown in the figure below. Which of the following expressions gives the distance, in meters, from the center of the kite to the ground?

A. $128\tan 64°$

B. $128\cos 64°$

C. $128\sin 64°$

D. $\dfrac{128}{\cos 64°}$

E. $\dfrac{128}{\sin 64°}$

53. In $\triangle XYZ$, the measure of $\angle X$ is 57°, the measure of $\angle Y$ is 72°, and the length of $\overline{XZ}$ is 12 inches. Which of the following is an expression for the length, in inches, of $\overline{YZ}$?

(Note: The law of sines states that for any triangle, the ratios of the lengths of the sides to the sines of the angles opposite those sides are equal.)

A. $\dfrac{\sin 57°}{12\sin 72°}$

B. $\dfrac{\sin 72°}{12\sin 57°}$

C. $\dfrac{12\sin 72°}{\sin 57°}$

D. $\dfrac{12\sin 57°}{\sin 72°}$

E. $\dfrac{(\sin 57°)\,(\sin 72°)}{12}$

56. Triangles $\triangle LMN$ and $\triangle WXY$ are shown below. The given side lengths are in inches. The area of $\triangle LMN$ is 40 square inches. What is the area of $\triangle WXY$, in square inches?

F. 15
G. 18
H. 20
J. 40
K. 45

58. The angle in the standard (x,y) coordinate plane shown below has its vertex at the origin. One side of this angle includes the positive x-axis, and the other side with measure θ passes through $(-12,-5)$. What is the sine of θ ?

F. $-\dfrac{13}{5}$

G. $-\dfrac{12}{13}$

H. $-\dfrac{5}{13}$

J. $\dfrac{5}{13}$

K. $\dfrac{12}{5}$

59. The domain of the function $f(x) = 4\sin(3x - 1) + 2$ is all real numbers. Which of the following is the range of the function $f(x)$?

A. $-4 \leq f(x) \leq 4$

B. $-6 \leq f(x) \leq 2$

C. $-5 \leq f(x) \leq 3$

D. $-2 \leq f(x) \leq 6$

E.   All real numbers

ANSWERS

Plane Geometry

6. F
14. H
20. H
24. J
27. C
31. B
37. E
48. G
54. F
55. D

Trigonometry

21. E
22. F
24. H
29. D
35. A
37. C
53. D
56. J
58. H
59. D

Coordinate Geometry

3. D
13. B
17. E
24. F
33. C
39. C
41. E
48. J
52. K
56. G

EXPLANATIONS

Plane Geometry

6. **F** The sum of the angles of a triangle is 180°, so $\angle X + \angle Z = 180° - 122° = 58°$. Congruent angles have equal measure so $\angle X$ and $\angle Z$ are each $\dfrac{58°}{2} = 29°$. Choice (J) neglects to divide the remaining measure by two. Choice (G) makes all three, rather than two, angles congruent. Choice (H) incorrectly assumes $\angle X$ is half of $\angle Y$. Choice (K) makes $\angle X$ congruent to $\angle Y$, rather than to $\angle Z$.

14. **H** Since the area of the six congruent squares is 96, the area of each square is $\dfrac{96}{6} = 16$. It might be tempting to select choice (F) here, but remember you're looking for the perimeter of the entire figure, not the area of each square. The area of a square is equal to s^2, so the length of the side of each square is $\sqrt{16} = 4$. The perimeter of the figure consists of 12 sides of congruent squares, so the perimeter is $12 \times 4 = 48$. Choice (G) confuses the sides of the square with the sides of the figure. Choice (J) misuses the fact that the figure is 8-sided; choice (K) finds the perimeter if all 4 sides of the 6 squares were exposed.

20. **H** Since N is the area of the larger triangle, we'll have to multiply by a fraction less than 1 to get a smaller area, eliminating choices (J) and (K). If we choose 5 for the height of both triangles and 8 for the base of the larger, the base of the smaller will be 2. Now the area of the smaller triangle is $\dfrac{1}{2}(2)(5) = 5$, and the area of the larger is $\dfrac{1}{2}(8)(5) = 20$, so choice (H) is correct—the smaller triangle's area is $\dfrac{1}{4}$ that of the larger. Careful—choices (F) and (G) incorrectly multiply and square the ratio of the side lengths.

24. **J** Carve up the weird figure into two rectangles. The larger rectangle has dimensions 9 meters by 12 meters. Since the left side of the figure is 4 more meters than the right side, the smaller rectangle must have dimensions 4 meters by 3 meters. Calculate the area of each rectangle: $A_L = 9 \times 12 = 108$ and $A_S = 4 \times 3 = 12$, then add find the total area: $108 + 12 = 120$. Choices (F), (G), and (H) are too small. Choice (K) finds the area of a 16×9 rectangle without the indentation.

27. **C** Given $\overline{GJ}$ is parallel to $\overline{FK}$, ΔFHK and ΔGHJ are similar triangles, so they have proportional sides. ΔGHJ is a right triangle, so you can either use the Pythagorean theorem or identify the sides as the Pythagorean triplet $6-8-10$ to determine $\overline{HJ}$ is 10. Then set up the proportion $\dfrac{\overline{FK}}{\overline{GJ}} = \dfrac{\overline{HK}}{\overline{HJ}}$ to determine $\overline{FK}$: $\dfrac{\overline{FK}}{6} = \dfrac{12}{8}$, so $\overline{FK}$ is 9 inches.

31. B   Use the figure to ballpark and eliminate choices (D) and (E). Plug in a value for the side lengths of square $JKLM$. If $\overline{JK}$ is 4 units, $\overline{KN}$ and $\overline{OK}$ are each 2 units and $\overline{ON}$ is $2\sqrt{2}$. Because $N, O, P,$ and Q are the midpoints of a square, $NOPQ$ is also a square with side lengths of $2\sqrt{2}$. Therefore, $\overline{NR}$ and $\overline{NS}$ are $\sqrt{2}$ and $\overline{RS}$ is $\sqrt{2}\left(\sqrt{2}\right) = 2$. Therefore, $\dfrac{JK}{RS} = \dfrac{4}{2} = 2$. Choice (A) compares a side of $JKLM$ to a side of $NOPQ$.

37. E   Use the circle area formula to determine the radius: $A = 36\pi = \pi r^2$. Because the radius of the circle is 6, the diameter $\overline{WY}$ is 12. $\overline{WY}$ is congruent to the side of the square, so the area of the square is $A = 12^2 = 144$. Choices (A) and (B) are the radius and diameter of the circle, not the area of the square. Choices (C) and (D) use the incorrect side lengths for the square.

48. G   Both $\overline{RX}$ and $\overline{SX}$ are radii of the circle, making them congruent. The triangle $\triangle RSX$, therefore, is isosceles, and $\angle SRX$ and $\angle RSX$ are congruent, each measuring 70°. The third angle $\angle RSX = 180° - 2(70°) = 40°$ and is equal to the measure of $\overset{\frown}{RS}$. Choices (J) and (K) make the incorrect pair of angles congruent.

54. F   Plug in values for the sides of the triangles: Triangle 1 can have a side length of 8 and triangle 2 can have a side length of 6, making $s = 2$. Equilateral triangles can be split into two 30°–60°–90° triangles, thus their altitudes are $\dfrac{1}{2}(\text{side length}) \times \sqrt{3}$. Triangle 1's altitude is $4\sqrt{3}$ and triangle 2's altitude is $6\sqrt{3}$, making the answer $4\sqrt{3} - 3\sqrt{3} = \sqrt{3}$. Choice (G) confuses 30°–60°–90° with 45°–45°–90°, and choices (H), (J), and (K) do not have a $\sqrt{3}$.

55. D $\overline{MN}$ and $\overline{OP}$ are the radii of their respective circles, so the radius $\overline{NY}$ of circle N is 10 inches and radius $\overline{OP}$ of circle O is 8 inches. Given $\overline{XY}$ is 3 inches long, $\overline{NX}$ is $10 - 3 = 7$ inches and $\overline{OY}$ is $8 - 3 = 5$ inches. Adding the three segments $\overline{NX}$, $\overline{XY}$, and $\overline{OY}$, the length of $\overline{NO}$ is $7 + 3 + 5 = 15$ inches. Choices (A) and (B) are too small, choice (C) calculates the length with $\overline{XY}$, and choice (E) doesn't consider the radii overlapping in $\overline{XY}$.

Coordinate Geometry

3. **D** To shift left, subtract from the x-coordinate: $5 - 3 = 2$; to shift up, add to the y-coordinate: $-4 + 6 = 2$. Choice (A) confuses the x- and y-coordinates, and choices (B), (C), and (E) confuse the addition and subtraction.

13. **B** The coordinates for midpoint are the averages of the endpoints: $\left[\dfrac{x_1 + x_2}{2}, \dfrac{y_1 + y_2}{2}\right]$. For segment $\overline{AB}$ the midpoint is at $\dfrac{6 + 10}{2} = 2, \dfrac{8 + 2}{2} = 5$. Choices (A) and (D) incorrectly take half the coordinate of one of the endpoints. Choice (C) adds, rather than averages, the endpoints. Choice (E) subtracts, rather than adds, the endpoint coordinates.

17. **E** The slope-intercept form is $y = mx + b$. Isolate the y variable by subtracting $5x$ and 2 from both sides of the equation to get $-y = -5x - 2$. Then divide both sides by -1 to get the slope-intercept equation $y = 5x + 2$. Choice (A) forgets to divide both sides by -1, choices (B) and (D) confuse the positive and negative signs, and choice (C) confuses the coefficient and constant values.

24. **F** Use the slope formula $\dfrac{y_2 - y_1}{x_2 - x_1} : \dfrac{8 - 3}{-3 - 5} = -\dfrac{5}{8}$. Choice (G) confuses the positive and negative signs; choices (H) and (J) add rather than subtract the coordinates; and choice (K) attempts to calculate $\dfrac{\text{run}}{\text{rise}}$.

33. **C** To determine the graph of the equation, you must isolate the y by subtracting $8x$ and dividing by 4. The resulting equation is $y = -2x + 3$, which is a line with a slope of -2 and the y-intercept of 3. Because the y-intercept is positive, the line crosses y-axis from Quadrant II to Quadrant I and extends into Quadrant IV. The line never passes through Quadrant III, eliminating choices (B), (D), and (E). Choice (A) is a partial answer and does not include Quadrant I. Alternatively, once the equation is in slope-intercept form, just plug it into your graphing calculator and look at the graph.

39. **C** Find the distance between the points using the distance formula: $d = \sqrt{(x_1 - x_2)^2 + (y_1 - y_2)^2} = \sqrt{[(-3) - (-6)]^2 + [(-5) - (-8)]^2} = \sqrt{(3)^2 + (3^2)} = \sqrt{18} = 3\sqrt{2}$. Multiply the coordinate distance by 20 to get the distance in kilometers. Choices (A) and (E) incorrectly calculate the distance by adding the coordinates and forgetting to square the differences, respectively. Choices (B) and (D) result when the distance formula is not used. If you have trouble remembering the distance formula, sketch a figure and use the Pythagorean theorem as detailed in the Introductory chapter.

41. **E** The graph crosses the x-axis when $y = 0$, and the x values at those points are called the solutions of the equation. Plug the solution values for x into the answers to determine which expressions give $y = 0$. Substituting $x = -3$, you can eliminate choices (A), (B), and (D) because they do not result in $y = 0$. Substituting $x = 6$, you can eliminate choice (C) because it does not result in $y = 0$.

48. J   For any function $f(x + h) + k$, h indicates horizontal shifts and k indicates vertical shifts. Because the horizontal shift is 4, not 3, you can eliminate choice (H). A negative h indicates a shift right, not left, eliminating choices (F) and (G). A negative k indicates a shift down, not up, eliminating choice (K).

52. K   The general equation of a circle is $(x - h)^2 + (y - k)^2 = r^2$, in which (h, k) is the center of the circle and r is the radius. Note that h and k are *subtracted* in the formula. Because the radius is 4, r^2 is 16, eliminating choices (F) and (G). Choices (H) and (J) confuse the signs of h and k.

56. G   The balloon remains stationary in the middle stage, so action (I) should be second in the order of events, eliminating choice (F). In the first stage, the graph is increasing which means the distance between the balloon and the ground increases, so the balloon is moving away, eliminating choices (H) and (K). The rate of increase is greater than the rate of decrease in the third stage, so choice (J) is incorrect. Only choice (G) gives the correct actions in the correct order.

Trigonometry

21. E   Draw a triangle and use SOHCAHTOA to label the known sides: leg $\overline{MN}$ is 3 and hypotenuse $\overline{LM}$ is 8. Use the Pythagorean theorem to determine the third side: $\overline{LN}^2 + 3^2 = 8^2$, so $\overline{LN} = \sqrt{55}$, eliminating choices (B) and (D). Since $\sin = \dfrac{\text{opposite}}{\text{adjacent}}$, $\sin M = \dfrac{\overline{LN}}{\overline{LM}} = \dfrac{\sqrt{55}}{8}$. Choice (A) gives $\csc M$, Choice (C) gives $\tan M$.

22. F   In SOHCAHTOA, Tan is Opposite over Adjacent relative to the angle, thus $\tan \theta = \dfrac{X}{Y}$. Choice (G) is $\sin \theta$; choice (H) is $\cos \theta$; choice (J) is $\cot \theta$; choice (K) is $\csc \theta$.

24. H   We know side adjacent the angle $8°$ and are trying to determine the side opposite the angle $8°$, so use TOA: $\tan 8° = \dfrac{x}{6}$, so $x = 6 \tan 8°$. Choices (F), (G), and (J) do not use tan, and choice (K) incorrectly calculates $6 \tan 82°$.

29. D   Because quadrilateral $GHJK$ has four right angles, it is a rectangle and $\overline{GK}$ measures 30 inches. We must use SOHCAHTOA to determine the side lengths of right triangle FGK, eliminating choices (A) and (B). Since we know the measure of $\angle F$, use SOH: $\sin 70° = \dfrac{30}{FK}$, which rearranges to give $\overline{FK} = \dfrac{30}{\sin 70°}$.

35. A   We know the side adjacent the angle θ and the hypotenuse, so use CAH to set up the problem: $\cos\theta = \dfrac{0.25}{1} = \dfrac{1}{4}$. To determine the measure of angle θ, use the inverse function $\cos^{-1}$, eliminating choices (B), (C), and (E). Choice (D) incorrectly uses the reciprocal of $\dfrac{\text{adjacent}}{\text{hypotenuse}}$.

37. C   The distance between the kite and the ground is opposite to the angle of $64°$. Since we also know the length of the hypotenuse, we're using SOH, eliminating choices (A), (B), and (D). Since $\sin 64° = \dfrac{\text{opposite}}{128}$, the distance is $128\sin 64°$. Choice (E) incorrectly sets up the ratio of sides.

53. D   Draw the triangle to determine that side $\overline{YZ}$ is opposite $\angle X$ and side $\overline{XZ}$ is opposite $\angle Y$. Using the law of sines, set up the proportion $\dfrac{12\text{ inches}}{\sin 72°} = \dfrac{\overline{YZ}}{\sin 57°}$. Multiply both sides by $\sin 57°$ to get $\overline{YZ} = \dfrac{12\sin 57°}{\sin 72°}$. Choice (C) does not use the correct angle-side pairs, and choices (A), (B), and (E) uses the incorrect proportions.

56. J   To determine the area of non-right triangles, use the formula $A = \dfrac{1}{2}ab\sin\theta$, in which θ is the angle between sides a and b. For ΔLMN, $A = 40 = \dfrac{1}{2}ab\sin 50°$, so $ab = 104.4$. Since ΔWXY has the same side lengths a and b, we can substitute $ab = 104.4$ for the area $A = \dfrac{1}{2}(ab)\sin 130°$. The area of ΔWXY is $\dfrac{1}{2}(104.4)(0.766) \approx 40$.

58. J   In the standard (x,y) coordinate plane, the sine of an angle in Quadrant II is always positive, eliminating choices (F), (G), and (H). Make a right triangle with the x-axis, which gives you a 5–12–13 triangle. The angle θ is at the origin, so the leg opposite the angle is 5 and the hypotenuse is 13. Sine is defined as opposite over hypotenuse, which in this case gives $\dfrac{5}{13}$, choice (J).

59. D   The range of $\sin x$ is normally between -1 to 1, inclusive; however, the range can change depending on the graph's amplitude and vertical shift. In the general form $A\sin(Bx + C) + D$, amplitude is indicated by A, vertical shift is indicated by D, and the range is between $-A + D$ and $A + D$. The range for this function, therefore, is $-4 + 2 \le f(x) \le 4 + 2$. Choice (A) neglects the vertical shift of the graph; choice (B) subtracts rather than adding the vertical shift of $+D$; choice (C) uses the horizontal rather than vertical shift value; choice (E) gives the domain, not the range of the function.

Comprehensive
Math Drill

ACT MATHEMATICS TEST

60 Minutes—60 Questions

DIRECTIONS: Solve each problem, choose the correct answer, and then darken the corresponding oval on your answer document.

Do not linger over problems that take too much time. Solve as many as you can; then return to the others in the time you have left for this test.

You are permitted to use a calculator on this test. You may use your calculator for any problems you choose, but some of the problems may best be done without using a calculator.

Note: Unless otherwise stated, all of the following should be assumed:

1. Illustrative figures are NOT necessarily drawn to scale.
2. Geometric figures lie in a plane.
3. The word *line* indicates a straight line.
4. The word *average* indicates arithmetic mean.

---

1. Bob's Burgers charges $8 dollars for a hamburger and $5 for an order of French fries. Last month, *h* hamburgers and *f* orders of fries were purchased. Which of the following expressions gives the total amount of money, in dollars, Bob's Burgers earned on hamburgers and fries last month?

   A. $5h + 8f$
   B. $8h + 5f$
   C. $13(h + f)$
   D. $40(h + f)$
   E. $8(h + f) + 5f$

2. If $a = 8$, $b = -2$, and $c = 3$, what does $(a - b + c)(b + c)$ equal?

   F. -65
   G. -13
   H. 9
   J. 13
   K. 65

3. An artist at the State Fair paints 40 portraits per day. A second artist paints 50 portraits per day. The second artist opens for business three days after the first. Both remain open until the Fair closes, which is 11 days after the first artist began. Together, the two artists have painted how many portraits?

   A. 400
   B. 440
   C. 720
   D. 840
   E. 900

4. Josh has been a professional baseball player for four years. His home run totals each year have been 30, 39, 51, and 44, respectively. In order to maintain his current average number of home runs per season, how many home runs must Josh hit next year?

   F. 31
   G. 39
   H. 41
   J. 44
   H. 51

DO YOUR FIGURING HERE.

GO ON TO THE NEXT PAGE.

5. A craftswoman is paid $9.00 per necklace for making up to 30 necklaces per week. For each necklace over 30 that she is asked to make in a week, she is paid 1.5 times her regular pay. How much does she earn in a week in which she is asked to make 34 necklaces?

A. $162
B. $270
C. $306
D. $324
E. $459

6. Which of the following mathematical expressions is equivalent to the verbal expression "The square root of a number, n, is 19 less than the value of 5 divided by n"?

F. $n^2 = \dfrac{5}{n} - 19$

G. $n^2 = \dfrac{n}{5} - 19$

H. $\sqrt{n} = 19 - \dfrac{n}{5}$

J. $\sqrt{n} = \dfrac{y}{n} - 19$

K. $\sqrt{n} = \dfrac{5}{n} - 19$

7. If $12(y - 3) = -7$, then $y = ?$

A. $-\dfrac{43}{12}$

B. $-\dfrac{10}{12}$

C. $-\dfrac{7}{12}$

D. $\dfrac{29}{12}$

E. $\dfrac{43}{12}$

8. At a department store, purses sell for $12 each during a one-day sale. Rita spent $84 on purses during the sale, $38.50 less than if she had bought the purses at the regular price. How much do purses cost at the regular price?

F. $ 5.50
G. $15.50
H. $16.00
J. $17.50
K. $20.00

GO ON TO THE NEXT PAGE.

9. $(2a - 5b^2)(2a + 5b^2) =$

- **A.** $4a^2 - 25b^4$
- **B.** $4a^2 - 10b^4$
- **C.** $4a^2 + 25b^4$
- **D.** $2a^2 - 25b^4$
- **E.** $2a^2 - 10b^4$

10. A rectangle's perimeter is 18 feet and its area is 18 square feet. What is the length of the longest side of the rectangle?

- **F.** 10
- **G.** 8
- **H.** 6
- **J.** 3
- **K.** 2

11. In $\triangle XYZ$, $\angle X$ is 64°. What is the sum of $\angle Y$ and $\angle Z$?

- **A.** 26°
- **B.** 64°
- **C.** 116°
- **D.** 126°
- **E.** 128°

12. Each morning, a glee club member chooses her outfit among 4 plaid skirts, 5 pairs of argyle socks, 3 sweaters, and 4 headbands. How many different outfits are possible for her to put together on any given morning consisting of one skirt, one pair of socks, one sweater, and one headband?

- **F.** 4
- **G.** 15
- **H.** 16
- **J.** 120
- **K.** 240

13. Positive integers x, y, and z are consecutive such that $x < y < z$. The sum of x, $2y$, and $\dfrac{z}{2}$ is 59. What are the values of x, y, and z, respectively?

- **A.** 10, 11, 12
- **B.** 11, 12, 13
- **C.** 14, 15, 16
- **D.** 16, 17, 18
- **E.** 18, 19, 20

14. A function $h(x)$ is defined as $h(x) = -5x^3$. What is $h(-2)$?

- **F.** −1,000
- **G.** −40
- **H.** 30
- **J.** 40
- **K.** 1,000

DO YOUR FIGURING HERE.

GO ON TO THE NEXT PAGE.

15. If $z = \sqrt[4]{97}$, then which of the following must be true?

    A. $2 < z < 3$
    B. $3 < z < 4$
    C. $4 < z < 5$
    D. $5 < z < 6$
    E. $6 < z$

DO YOUR FIGURING HERE.

16. What is the greatest common factor of 96, 108, and 144 ?

    F. 12
    G. 18
    H. 24
    J. 36
    K. 48

17. Cowan Cola is holding a contest to develop a new, more environmentally efficient can for its soft drink. The winning can is a cylinder ten inches tall, with a volume of 40π in³. What is the radius, in inches, of the can?

    A. 1
    B. 2
    C. 4
    D. 5
    E. 8

18. A clock has 12 numbered points. Four points W, X, Y, Z lie on the clock representing certain numbers. W represents 3:00. X is 4 units clockwise from W. Y is 9 units counterclockwise from W. Z is 5 units counterclockwise from W and 7 units clockwise from W. What is the order of points, starting with W and working clockwise around the circle?

    F. W, X, Y, Z
    G. W, X, Z, Y
    H. W, Y, X, Z
    J. W, Y, Z, X
    K. W, Z, Y, X

19. Tribbles reproduce at a rate described by the function $f(a) = 12(3)^a$, here a represents the number of days and $f(a)$ represents the number of tribbles. At this rate, how many tribbles will there be at the end of Day Four?

    A. 48
    B. 96
    C. 240
    D. 972
    E. 1,296

GO ON TO THE NEXT PAGE.

20. The height of a triangle is half the height of a larger triangle. The two triangles have the same base. The area of the larger triangle is Y square feet. The area of the smaller triangle is xY square units. Which of the following is the value of x?

F. $\dfrac{1}{4}$

G. $\dfrac{1}{2}$

H. 1

J. 2

K. 4

DO YOUR FIGURING HERE.

21. $(2x + 3y + 4z) - (6x - 7y + 8z)$ is equivalent to:

A. $-4x + 10y - 4z$

B. $-4x + 10y + 12z$

C. $-4x - 4y - 4z$

D. $-8x + 10y + 12z$

E. $-8x - 4y + 12z$

22. The right triangle shown below has lengths measured in inches. What is $\cos\theta$?

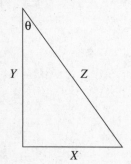

F. $\dfrac{X}{Y}$

G. $\dfrac{X}{Z}$

H. $\dfrac{Y}{X}$

J. $\dfrac{Y}{Z}$

K. $\dfrac{Z}{Y}$

GO ON TO THE NEXT PAGE.

23. On a dead-end street, 8 houses are evenly spaced around a circular cul-de-sac. A newspaper delivery person bikes around the cul-de-sac and tosses the newspapers onto the driveway of each house. The delivery person bikes rapidly enough that the person can only toss to every third house. On which lap around the cul-de-sac will the delivery person have delivered newspapers to all 8 houses on the street?

A. 2nd
B. 3rd
C. 4th
D. 8th
E. 11th

DO YOUR FIGURING HERE.

24. Lines q and m are in the standard (x,y) coordinate plane. The equation for line q is $y = 23x + 500$. The y-intercept of line m is 10 less than the y-intercept of line q. What is the y-intercept of line m ?

F. 2.3
G. 13
H. 50
J. 490
K. 510

25. The expression $-9a^5(8a^7 - 4a^3)$ is equivalent to:

A. $-36a^9$
B. $-72a^{12} + 36a^8$
C. $-72a^{12} - 36a^8$
D. $-72a^{35} + 36a^{15}$
E. $-72a^{35} - 36a^{15}$

26. $-4|-9 + 2| = ?$

F. -44
G. -28
H. 3
J. 28
K. 44

GO ON TO THE NEXT PAGE.

DO YOUR FIGURING HERE.

27. In right triangle $\triangle WYZ$ shown below, $\overline{XV}$ is perpendicular to $\overline{WZ}$ at point V and is parallel to $\overline{YZ}$. Line segments $\overline{WY}$, $\overline{XV}$, and $\overline{WV}$ measure 30 inches, 6 inches, and 8 inches, respectively. What is the measurement, in inches, of $\overline{YZ}$?

    A. 15
    B. 18
    C. 20
    D. 24
    E. 27

28. As an experiment in botany class, students tracked a plant growing at a constant rate upward perpendicular to the ground. As shown in the table below, they measured the height, h inches, of the plant at 1-week intervals from $w = 0$ weeks to $w = 4$ weeks.

w	0	1	2	3	4
h	7	10	13	16	19

Which of the following equations expresses this data?

    F. $h = w + 7$
    G. $h = 3w + 4$
    H. $h = 3w + 7$
    J. $h = 7w + 3$
    K. $h = 10w$

29. The inequality $4(n - 3) < 5(n + 2)$ is equivalent to which of the following inequalities?

    A. $n > -22$
    B. $n > -14$
    C. $n > -13$
    D. $n > -2$
    E. $n > 2$

GO ON TO THE NEXT PAGE.

30. The sides of an equilateral triangle are 4 inches long. One vertex of the triangle is at (1,1) on a coordinate graph labeled in inch units. Which of the following could give the coordinates of another vertex of the triangle?

   F. (−4, 1)
   G. (0, 1)
   H. (2, 3)
   J. (1,−3)
   K. (5,−3)

DO YOUR FIGURING HERE.

31. For $\triangle LMN$, shown below, which of the following expresses the value of m in terms of n ?

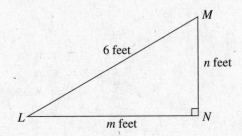

   A. $6 - n$
   B. $\sqrt{6 - n}$
   C. $\sqrt{12 + n^2}$
   D. $\sqrt{36 - n^2}$
   E. $\sqrt{36 + n^2}$

32. A jar holds 10 pear jellybeans, 16 cherry jellybeans, and 19 watermelon jellybeans. How many extra pear jellybeans must be added to the 45 jellybeans currently in the jar so that the probability of randomly selecting a pear jellybean is $\frac{3}{8}$?

   F. 9
   G. 11
   H. 21
   J. 35
   K. 45

GO ON TO THE NEXT PAGE.

33. The graph of the equation $6x + 3y = 12$ is found in which quadrants of the standard (x,y) coordinate plane below?

DO YOUR FIGURING HERE.

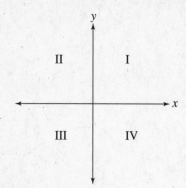

A. II and IV only
B. I, II, and III only
C. I, II, and IV only
D. I, III, and IV only
E. II, III, and IV only

34. The graph of $y = -2x^2 + 10$ contains the point $(3, 4n)$ in the standard (x,y) coordinate plane. What is the value of n ?

F.   7
G.   1
H. −2
J. −4
K. −8

35. Jennifer, Kelly, and Meredith split their apartment rent. Jennifer paid $\frac{2}{3}$ of the rent, Kelly paid $\frac{1}{4}$ of the rent, and Meredith paid the rest. What is the ratio of Jennifer's contribution to Kelly's contribution to Meredith's contribution?

A.   1:3:8
B.   3:8:1
C.   3:1:8
D.   8:3:1
E.   8:1:3

GO ON TO THE NEXT PAGE.

36. In the standard (x,y) coordinate plane, a circle has an equation of $x^2 + (y+4)^2 = 28$. Which of the following gives the center and radius of the circle, in coordinate units?

	center	radius
F.	$(0, -4)$	$\sqrt{28}$
G.	$(0, -4)$	14
H.	$(0, -4)$	28
J.	$(0, \ \ 4)$	$\sqrt{28}$
K.	$(0, \ \ 4)$	14

37. An equilateral triangle and 2 semicircles have dimensions as shown in the figure below. What is the perimeter, in inches, of the figure?

6 in

- **A.** $3 + 3\pi$
- **B.** $6 + 6\pi$
- **C.** $6 + 12\pi$
- **D.** $18 + 6\pi$
- **E.** $18 + 12\pi$

38. In the figure below, points H, J, K, and L bisect the sides of rhombus $DEFG$, and point M is the intersection of $\overline{HK}$ and $\overline{JL}$. The area enclosed by $DEFG$ except the area enclosed by $HEFM$ is shaded. What is the ratio of the area of $HEFM$ to the area of the shaded area?

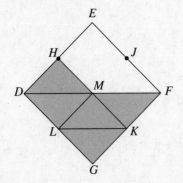

- **F.** 1:2
- **G.** 3:4
- **H.** 3:5
- **J.** 3:8
- **K.** Cannot be determined from the given information

GO ON TO THE NEXT PAGE.

39. In the standard (x,y) coordinate plane, the endpoints of $\overline{FG}$ lie on the coordinates $(-6,10)$ and $(8,-2)$. What is the y-coordinate of the midpoint of $\overline{FG}$?

A. 1
B. 2
C. 4
D. 6
E. 8

DO YOUR FIGURING HERE.

40. What is the volume, in cubic feet, of a cube with a side of length 9 feet?

F. 729
G. 486
J. 243
H. 81
K. 27

41. The system below has linear equations, in which r, s, t, and v are positive integers.

$$rx + sy = t$$

$$rx + sy = v$$

Which of the following best describes a possible graph of such a system of equations in the standard (x,y) coordinate plane?

   I.   2 lines intersecting at only 1 point
  II. 1 single line
 III. 2 parallel lines

A. I only
B. III only
C. I and II only
D. II and III only
E. I and III only

GO ON TO THE NEXT PAGE.

42. Given the dimensions in the figure below, which of the following expresses the distance, in feet, from the tree to the house?

F. $40 \sin 34°$

G. $40 \cos 34°$

H. $40 \tan 34°$

J. $\dfrac{40}{\sin 34°}$

K. $\dfrac{40}{\cos 34°}$

43. The chart below shows the percentage of students, by grade, enrolled in a school. A student is picked randomly in a lottery to win a new graphing calculator. What are the odds (in the grade:not in the grade) that the winning student is in Grade 6 ?

Grade	5	6	7	8	9
Percentage of total number of students	12	22	25	27	14

A. 1:4
B. 1:5
C. 7:25
D. 11:39
E. 11:50

GO ON TO THE NEXT PAGE.

Use the following information to answer questions 44–46.

The figure below shows the pattern of a square tile mosaic to decorate the wall of Chelsea's Mexican Café. Grout fills the small spaces between individual tile pieces. All white triangular tiles are equilateral and share a vertex with each adjacent triangular piece. A green square piece is at the center of the mosaic. The length of the mosaic is 3 meters.

44. How many lines of symmetry in the plane does the pattern of the tile mosaic have?

   F. 2
   G. 3
   H. 4
   J. 8
   K. Infinitely many

45. What is the length of the diagonal of the mosaic, to the nearest 0.1 meters?

   A. 2.4
   B. 3.0
   C. 3.4
   D. 4.2
   E. 5.7

46. Joe wants to put a tile mosaic on the wall of his office. The pattern of the mosaic will be identical to that in the restaurant. The length of the office wall is 20% shorter than the length of the mosaic. The office wall is how many meters long?

   F. 0.6
   G. 2.4
   H. 2.8
   J. 3.6
   K. 6.0

GO ON TO THE NEXT PAGE.

DO YOUR FIGURING HERE.

47. In the figure below, $\overline{DE} \parallel \overline{FG}$, $\overline{DG}$ bisects $\angle HDE$, and $\overline{HG}$ bisects $\angle FGD$. If the measure of $\angle EDG$ is 68°, what is the measure of $\angle DHG$?

A. 68°
B. 78°
C. 80°
D. 82°
E. Cannot be determined from the given information

48. In the figure shown below, points A, B, and C lie on the circle with an area of 16π square meters and center O (not shown). $\overline{AC}$ is the longest chord in the circle, and the measure of $\overline{AB}$ is 4 meters. What is the degree measure of minor arc BC ?

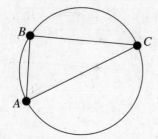

F. 60°
G. 90°
H. 120°
J. 145°
K. Cannot be determined from the given information

49. For which of the following values of b would the system of equations below have no solutions?

$$12x + 8y = 16$$

$$3x + by = 2$$

A. 2
B. 4
C. 8
D. 16
E. 32

GO ON TO THE NEXT PAGE.

DO YOUR FIGURING HERE.

Use the following information to answer questions 50–52.

Rebecca and Scott make and sell pies and cookies for school bake sales. It takes them 1 hour to make a dozen cookies and 3 hours to make a pie. The shaded triangular region shown below is the graph of a system of inequalities representing school-week constraints Rebecca and Scott have on their baking. For making and selling d dozen cookies and p pies, they make a profit of $12d + 25p$ dollars. They sell all the goods they bake.

50. The constraint represented by the horizontal line segment containing (9,1) means that each school-week Rebecca and Scott make a minimum of:

    F. 1 pie
    G. 9 pies
    H. 1 dozen cookies
    J. 9 dozen cookies
    K. 10 dozen cookies

51. What is the maximum profit Rebecca and Scott can earn from the baking they do in 1 school-week?

    A. $100
    B. $109
    C. $122
    D. $133
    E. $237

52. During the third week of October each year, school is closed for Fall Break, and Rebecca and Scott have more time than usual to bake. During that week, for every hour that they spend baking, they donate $2 to the school's fund for after-school reading programs. This year, they baked 5 pies and 3 dozen cookies during Fall Break. Which of the following is closest to the percent of that week's profit they donated to the reading program fund?

    F. 5%
    G. 9%
    H. 15%
    J. 18%
    K. 22%

GO ON TO THE NEXT PAGE.

DO YOUR FIGURING HERE.

53. The *determinant* of a matrix $\begin{bmatrix} a & c \\ b & d \end{bmatrix}$ equals $ad - bc$. What must be the value of w for the matrix $\begin{bmatrix} w & w \\ w & 10 \end{bmatrix}$ to have a determinant of 25 ?

   A. 5

   B. $\dfrac{10}{3}$

   C. $\dfrac{5}{2}$

   D. $-\dfrac{5}{3}$

   E. -5

54. Henry discovers that the population of the bacterial colony in his lab can be calculated using the equation $x = B(1 + .2g)^n$ where x is the current population, B is the original number of bacteria, g is a growth rate constant for that species, and n is the number of days elapsed. Which of the following is an expression for B in terms of g, n, and x ?

   F. $x - .2g^n$

   G. $x + .2g^n$

   H. $\left(\dfrac{x}{1 + .2g} \right)^n$

   J. $\dfrac{x}{(1 - .2g)^n}$

   K. $\dfrac{x}{(1 + .2g)^n}$

55. If m and n are real numbers such that $m < -1$ and $n > 1$, then which of the following inequalities *must* be true?

   A. $\dfrac{n}{m} > 1$

   B. $|n|^2 > |m|$

   C. $\dfrac{n}{7} + 2 > \dfrac{m}{7} + 2$

   D. $n^2 + 1 > m^2 + 1$

   E. $n^{-2} > m^{-2}$

GO ON TO THE NEXT PAGE.

56. Triangles *TVW* and *XYZ* are shown below. The given side lengths are in inches. The area of $\triangle TVW$ is 45 square inches. What is the area of $\triangle XYZ$ in square inches?

DO YOUR FIGURING HERE.

F. 22.5
G. 27
H. 30
J. 45
K. 50

57. Triangle *JKL* is shown in the figure below. The measure of $\angle K$ is 50°, $JK = 9$ cm, and $KL = 6$ cm. Which of the following is the lengths, in centimeters, of *LJ* ?

(Note: For a triangle with sides of length *a*, *b*, and *c* opposite angles $\angle A$, $\angle B$, and $\angle C$, respectively, the law of sines states $\dfrac{\sin \angle A}{a} = \dfrac{\sin \angle B}{b} = \dfrac{\sin \angle C}{c}$ and the law of cosines states $c^2 = a^2 + b^2 - 2ab\cos \angle C$.)

A. $9 \sin 50°$

B. $6 \sin 50°$

C. $\sqrt{9^2 - 6^2}$

D. $\sqrt{9^2 + 6}$

E. $\sqrt{9^2 + 6^2 - 2(9)(6)\cos 50°}$

58. What is the sum of the first 3 terms of the arithmetic sequence in which the 7th term is 13.5 and the 11th term is 18.3 ?

F. 15.9
G. 22.5
H. 25.5
J. 32.4
K. 43.5

GO ON TO THE NEXT PAGE.

59. In the equation $w^2 - pw + q = 0$, p and q are integers. The *only* possible value for w is 8. What is the value of p ?

    A.   8
    B. −8
    C. 16
    D. −16
    E. 64

60. The solution set of which of the following equations is the set of real numbers that are 4 units from −1 ?

    F. $|x + 1| = 4$

    G. $|x - 1| = 4$

    H. $|x + 4| = 1$

    J. $|x - 4| = 1$

    K. $|x + 4| = -1$

DO YOUR FIGURING HERE.

END OF TEST.
STOP! DO NOT TURN THE PAGE UNTIL TOLD TO DO SO.

ANSWERS

1. B	31. D
2. J	32. G
3. D	33. C
4. H	34. H
5. D	35. D
6. K	36. F
7. D	37. B
8. J	38. H
9. A	39. C
10. H	40. F
11. C	41. D
12. K	42. F
13. D	43. D
14. J	44. H
15. B	45. D
16. F	46. G
17. B	47. B
18. H	48. H
19. D	49. A
20. G	50. F
21. A	51. B
22. J	52. K
23. B	53. A
24. J	54. K
25. B	55. C
26. G	56. J
27. B	57. E
28. H	58. G
29. A	59. C
30. J	60. F

EXPLANATIONS

1. **B** Since h represents the number of hamburgers, multiply it by \$8 to get the total amount of money paid for burgers; since f represents the number of orders of fries, multiply it by \$5 to get the total amount of money paid for fries. You want the total amount of money earned, so you need to add the two expressions together: $8h + 5f$. You can also just plug in values for h and f and see which answer choice matches the target answer you get for those values—only choice (B) will work for all values of h and f.

2. **J** Plug in the values given in the question. The problem should then read $(8 -[-2] + 3)(-2 + 3)$. Follow the order of operations and do the arithmetic within each parenthesis individually before multiplying: $(13)(1) = 13$.

3. **D** Figure out the two artists separately, and then combine. The first one paints 40 portraits a day for 11 days, so 440 total. The second paints 50 per day for 8 days, so 400 total. Add them up, and there are 840 portraits.

4. **H** If you add together all the home runs, you get 164. Divide that by four seasons and his average number of home runs per season is 41. The question is simply asking you how to keep a 41 home run average going after a fifth year. Simple: Hit 41 home runs exactly in year five.

5. **D** The trick here is that you must calculate the first 30 necklaces at the regular rate of \$9.00 each: She makes \$270 for the first 30. Then figure out what 1.5 times her usual rate is (it's \$13.50) and multiply that by the extra four necklaces. She gets \$54 for the extras; add that to the \$270, and she makes a total of \$324 for the week.

6. **K** This question is about translating English into math. The trickiest part is remembering to subtract 19 from $\dfrac{5}{n}$ instead of the other way around. Read closely and make sure you take the square root and not the square of n.

7. **D** Those answer choices are ugly, but if you have a good calculator and are comfortable with all the fractions and parentheses, you can PITA. Otherwise, just solve for the variable. First, distribute the 12 on the left side, and you get $12y - 36 = -7$. Add 36 to both sides and you get $12y = 29$. Divide both sides by 12, and you're done.

8. **J** First, calculate how many \$12 purses you get for \$84—you can buy seven of them. The difference between the prices is \$38.50, so divide this by 7, and you get the value of the discount per purse, which turns out to be \$5.50. Now add that to the sale price of a single purse, and you get \$17.50 as the non-discount price.

9. A   You can Plug In, though the numbers will get fairly large once you start taking things to the 4th power. Or you can solve it as a quadratic, using FOIL. You may recognize it as a twist on $(x + y)(x - y)$. You know that when one binomial is a sum and the other a difference, their product will be the difference of two squares, so eliminate choice (C). After that, just make sure everything gets squared, coefficients as well as variables, and you wind up with choice (A).

10. H   The formula for a rectangle's area is base × height. PITA to find which answer choice fits the parameters in the question. Remember to start with the middle value! If we use 6 for the longer side of the rectangle, that means the short side will be 3, since we need an area of 18. Adding all four sides together gives us $6 + 6 + 3 + 3 = 18$, the perimeter given in the question, so choice (H) is the correct answer.

11. C   The sum of all the angles in any triangle is 180. Since $\angle X$ is 64°, the sum of $\angle Y$ and $\angle Z$ is calculated by subtracting 64° from 180°, leaving 116°.

12. K   Every possibility must be accounted for. For each of the four skirts, there are five sock options. $4 \times 5 = 20$, so there are 20 skirt/sock combinations. For each of those 20 combinations, there are three sweater options. $20 \times 3 = 60$, so there are 60 skirt/sock/sweater combinations. Finally, for each of these 60 combinations, there are 4 headband options. $60 \times 4 = 240$ total outfit combinations.

13. D   Use PITA. Start with the middle answer, choice (C), and you'll get $14 + 2(15) + \dfrac{16}{2} = 52$, so you know you need a higher set of numbers. Go to choice (D), and you'll get $16 + 2(17) + \dfrac{18}{2} = 59$.

14. J   When ACT gives you a function and then identifies a number inside the parentheses, it means to plug that number in for x every time it appears in the question. In this case, $x = -2$, so the function will end up reading $h(x) = -5(-2)^3$. Then you get $h(x) = -5(-2)^3$. $(-2)^3 = -8$, and when you multiply that by –5, you get 40. Watch out for the traps in choices (J) and (K), which involve cubing the –5 along with the x.

15. B   Don't overcomplicate here. Grab your calculator and see what the 4th root of 97 is (it's in the "Math" menu of your TI 80-series calculator). Another approach would be to recognize that $z = \sqrt[4]{97}$ could be altered to read $z^4 = 97$. This way, you can PITA. Since $3^4 = 81$, and $4^4 = 256$, the value of z must be between 3 and 4.

16. F   The simplest approach is to PITA. Grab your calculator and divide each of the numbers in the question by each answer choice, starting with the highest answer choice, since the question asks for the greatest. 24 and 48 are factors of 96 and 144, but not of 108, so choices (H) and (K) must be eliminated. 18 and 36 are factors of 108 and 144, but not of 96, so choices (G) and (J) must be eliminated. That leaves choice (F) as the correct answer, because 12 divides evenly into all three numbers.

17. **B** You'll need to know the formula for volume of a cylinder: $V = \pi r^2 h$. So plug the known height (10") into the formula and set it equal to the known volume. $40\pi = \pi r^2 (10)$. $6\pi = \pi r^2 (4)$. Solve from here, and you will find that $r = 2$. You can also PITA, since the answer choices represent the radius in that formula.

18. **H** This problem is very difficult to visualize, so make sure you draw a figure. Since W represents 3:00, count the hours in the directions indicated in the problem and mark the points that you reach. X will be 7:00; Y will be 6:00, and Z will be 10:00. So the order, clockwise, will be W, Y, X, Z.

19. **D** The trouble with this problem is that it looks more complicated than it is. Since a represents the number of days and the problem asks you about Day Four, plug 4 in for a and solve the equation. 3^4 is 81 and 81(12) is 972 tribbles.

20. **G** The best approach is to Plug In. You need the formula for area of a triangle: $\frac{1}{2}bh$. The two triangles have the same base, so start there—plug in 5, for instance. Then Plug In for the heights; try 4 for the larger and 2 for the smaller. Now you can compute the respective areas. For the larger, $\frac{1}{2}(5)(4) = 10$ square feet (the problem calls this y), and for the smaller, $\frac{1}{2}(5)(2) = 5$ square feet. So the final step is to re-read the problem and make sure what you're being asked for. $Y = 10$, and $xY = 5$, so $x = \frac{1}{2}$.

21. **A** To simplify the expression, distribute the negative to every term in the second set of variables and drop the parentheses: $2x + 3y + 4z - 6x + 7y - 8z$. Combine like terms to get $-4x + 10y - 4z$. Choices (B), (C), (D), and (E) forget to distribute the negative to at least one of the terms.

22. **J** Use SOHCAHTOA for right triangles: CAH means $\cos \theta = \dfrac{adjacent}{hypotenuse}$, which is $\dfrac{y}{z}$. Remember to identify the adjacent and opposite legs of the triangle relative to angle θ. Choice (G) incorrectly gives the adjacent leg as x rather than y; choice (F) gives $\tan \theta$; choice (H) gives $\cot \theta$; choice (K) gives $\sec \theta$.

23. **B** Draw a diagram with numbers 1–8 evenly spaced around a circle. On the first run, the paper is delivered to houses 1, 4, and 7; on the second run, the paper is delivered to houses 2, 5, and 8; on the third run, the paper is delivered to houses 3 and 6. Therefore, by the third lap, the paper has been delivered to all the houses.

24. **J** In the equation of a line $y = mx + b$, the y-intercept is given by constant b, thus line q has a y-intercept of 500. The y-intercept of line m is 10 less than line q, so subtract 10 from 500 to get 490. Choice (K) incorrectly adds 10; choice (H) calculates the y-intercept as 10 *times* less, rather than 10 less than that of line m. Choices (F) and (G) use the slope rather than the y-intercept.

25. B   Simplify the expression by multiplying $-9a^5$ to each term in the parentheses. Remember MADSPM. When bases are multiplied, exponents are added. Therefore, the equation should look like this: $-9a^5(8a^7 - 4a^3) = -72a^{(5+7)} + 36a^{(5+3)} = -72a^{12} + 36a^8$. Choices (D) and (E) incorrectly multiply the exponents. Choice (C) doesn't distribute the negative sign to the second term. Choice (A) incorrectly subtracts non-combinable terms inside the parentheses and then multiplies $-9a^5$.

26. G   Consider PEMDAS and first combine the terms inside the absolute value: $-4|-9+2| = -4|-7|$. Then take the absolute value of -7, which is $+7$, and multiply by -4 to get -28. Choices (F) and (K) incorrectly take the absolute value of -9 and 2 first and then combine. Choice (H) adds rather than multiplying -4 and $+7$. Choice (J) neglects to take the absolute value of -7.

27. B   Given YZ is parallel to XV, $\triangle WXV$ and $\triangle WYZ$ are similar triangles, thus they have proportional sides. First use Pythagorean theorem $WX^2 = 6^2 + 8^2$ to calculate WX is 10, or remember that this is one of the special right triangles. Then set up the proportion $\dfrac{WX}{WY} = \dfrac{XV}{YZ}$ to find YZ: $\dfrac{10}{30} = \dfrac{6}{YZ}$, and YZ is 18 inches. Choices (A), (C), and (E) do not use the correct proportions; choice (D) is the length of WZ, not YZ.

28. H   Plug in a w value from the table and eliminate equations that do not give the corresponding h value. When you plug in $w = 0$, choices (G), (J), and (K) do not give $h = 7$. When you plug in $w = 1$, choice (F) gives $h = 8$, not 10, and also can be eliminated.

29. A   Simplify the expression by distributing the coefficients on both sides of the inequality: $4(n-3) < 5(n+2)$ becomes $4n - 12 < 5n + 10$. Combine like terms to get $-n < 22$ and divide by -1, remembering to flip the inequality sign. Choices (B), (C), (D), and (E) all result from either neglecting to distribute the coefficient completely through the parentheses or mixing up the positive and negative signs.

30. J   The other vertices of the triangle must be 4 inches from $(1,1)$. Use POE. Choice (F) is 5 units to the left and choice (G) is only 1 unit to the left. Using either right triangles or distance formula, you can determine choice (H) is not long enough and choice (K) is too long. Choice (J) is 4 units due south from $(1,1)$. If you have trouble remembering the distance formula, just sketch and ballpark!

31. D   Use the Pythagorean theorem: $m^2 + n^2 = 6^2$. Isolate m by subtracting n^2 and square rooting both sides. Choices (A), (B), and (C) do not correctly square each side length before isolating m. Choice (E) treats side m as the hypotenuse rather than one of the legs of the right triangle. If you get stuck with the algebra, plug in a value for n and use your calculator.

32. G   Probability is the fraction of what you want (pear jellybeans) over total number of possibilities (all jellybeans). Use PITA. There are currently $10 + 16 + 19 = 45$ jellybeans in the jar. Start with choice (H). If 21 pear jellybeans are added, then there will be a total of 66 jellybeans in the jar. The probability of selecting a pear jellybean will be $\frac{21}{66}$, which is too low. Go to choice (G). If 11 jellybeans are added, there will be a total of 56 jellybeans in the jar. The probability of selecting a pear jellybeans will be $\frac{21}{56}$, which simplifies to $\frac{3}{8}$, making choice (G) the correct answer.

33. C   To determine the graph of the equation, you must isolate the y by subtracting $6x$ *and* dividing by 3. The resulting equation is $y = -2x + 4$, which is a line with a slope of -2 and the y-intercept of $+4$. Because the y-intercept is positive, the line crosses y-axis from Quadrant II to Quadrant I and extends into Quadrant IV. The line never passes through Quadrant II, eliminating choices (B), (D), and (E). Choice (A) is a partial answer and does not include Quadrant I. Remember, in order to avoid doing any figuring, once you've got the equation in slope-intercept form, you can just plug it in to your graphing calculator.

34. H   Substitute the values $(3, 4n)$ in for (x, y) in the equation to get $4n = -2(3)^2 + 10$. Remember PEMDAS: $4n = -2(9) + 10$, so $4n = -8$ and $n = -2$. Choice (F) results when you mix up the positive and negative signs. Choices (G) and (J) result when you do not use PEMDAS correctly. Choice (K) is a partial answer and gives the value of $4n$, not n.

35. D   Plug In! Make sure you choose a value for the rent that divides evenly by 3 and 4. Let's say the rent is $24. Then, Jennifer pays $16, Kelly pays $6, and Meredith pays the remainder, or $2. The ratio of Jennifer's contribution to Kelly's contribution to Meredith's contribution is then 16:6:2, which simplifies to 8:3:1, or choice (D).

36. F   The general equation of a circle is $(x - h)^2 + (y - k)^2 = r^2$, for which (h, k) are the coordinates for the center of the circle and r gives the radius length. For the given equation, the $h = 0$ and $k = -4$; choices (J) and (K) confuse the sign in front of k. Since $r^2 = 28$, the radius of the circle is $\sqrt{28}$. Choice (G) divides by 2 rather than square rooting 28. Choice (H) gives the value of r^2, not r.

37. B   The perimeter of the figure consists of one side of the equilateral triangle and the arc length of two semicircles. You can immediately eliminate choices (A), (D), and (E) because the length of one side of the equilateral triangle is 6 inches. Both semicircles have a diameter of 6 and given $C = d\pi = 6\pi$, each semicircle has an arc length of 3π. With the exposed side of the triangle, the perimeter of the figure should be $P = 6 + 3\pi + 3\pi = 6 + 6\pi$. If you selected choice (C), you may have found the circumferences of two full circles rather than two semicircles.

38. H   Because *DEFG* is a rhombus, which has equal sides and equal angles, all 8 triangles formed by drawing the diagonals in the figure are equivalent. *HEFM* encloses the area of 3 triangles and the shaded region the area of 5 triangles, thus the ratio is 3:5. Choice (J) is the ratio of the unshaded area to the total area.

39. C The midpoint is the average of the endpoints, so the y-coordinate of the midpoint is $\dfrac{y_1 + y_2}{2} = \dfrac{10 + (-2)}{2} = 4$. Choice (A) is the x-coordinate of the midpoint. Choices (B) and (E) only find the sum of the endpoint coordinates. Choice (D) confuses the negative sign and finds the average of 10 and 2.

40. F The volume of a cube is s^3, so this cube is $9^3 = 729$ cubic feet. Choice (G) gives the surface area of the cube. Choice (J) the area of 3 faces of the cube, choice (H) gives the area of 1 face, and choice (J) confuses the side as 3 feet rather than 9.

41. D Rearrange both equations into $y = mx + b$ form to compare their slopes and y-intercepts. The first equation $rx + sy = t$ becomes $y = -\dfrac{r}{s}x + \dfrac{t}{s}$. The second equation, $rx + sy = v$, becomes $y = -\dfrac{r}{s}x + \dfrac{v}{s}$. Both functions have the slope of $-\dfrac{r}{s}$ so they cannot intersect at only 1 point, eliminating Roman numeral I, thus choices (A), (C), and (E). A system of two linear functions can give a single line graph if the equations have the same slope and y-intercept, which occurs if $t = v$. Lines with same slope and different y-intercepts are parallel and never intersect so when t and v are not equal, you'll get two parallel lines, thus the answer must be choice (D).

42. F Because you are finding the side *O*pposite the 34° angle and are given the *H*ypotenuse, use SOHcahtoa or the *sine* function, eliminating choices (G), (H), and (K). Since $\sin 34° = \dfrac{\text{opposite}}{40}$, you solve for the distance by multiplying 40, not dividing and thus eliminating choice (J).

43. D Because 6th graders comprise 22% of the total number of students, $100 - 22 = 78\%$ of the students are not in 6th grade. The odds is the ratio of 22:78, which reduces to 11:39. Choice (E) incorrectly calculates the ratio of 6th graders to the total number of students. Choices (A), (B), and (C) are approximations of 22%; however, not as accurate as choice (D).

44. H Lines of symmetry cut the figure into two mirror images.

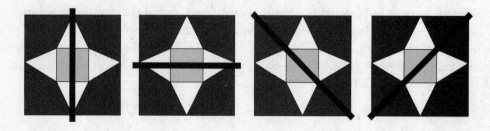

Since each of the divisions above creates two mirror images, the figure has four lines of symmetry.

45. **D** Because a square has right angles, you can determine the diagonal length using the Pythagorean theorem: $3^2 + 3^2 = d^2$. The diagonal is $3\sqrt{2}$ meters ≈ 4.2 meters. Choices (A) and (C) take the square root of 6 and 12, rather than 18. Choices (B) and (E) incorrectly calculate the diagonal without the Pythagorean theorem.

46. **G** Because the office wall is shorter, you can eliminate choices (J) and (K) immediately. Calculate 20% of the length of the current mosaic: 0.20×3 meters $= 0.6$ meters. Since the length is 20% shorter, subtract 0.6 meters from the original 3 meters. Choice (F) is a partial answer, but does not give the actual length of the office wall. Choice (G) subtracts 0.2 rather than 20%.

47. **B** Because $\overline{DG}$ bisects $\angle HDE$, $\angle HDG = \angle EDG = 68°$. Since $\overline{DE} \parallel \overline{FG}$, $\angle FGD = \angle EDG = 68°$. Since $\overline{HG}$ bisects $\angle FGD$, $\angle DGH = 34°$. $\angle DHG + \angle HDG + \angle DGH = 180°$, thus $\angle DHG = 78°$.

48. **H** Given the area of the circle is 16π square meters, the radius is 4 meters. $\overline{AC}$ is the longest chord in the circle, which is the diameter of the circle, so O can be labeled as the midpoint. $\overline{OA}$ and $\overline{OB}$ are each 4 meters, so $\triangle OAB$ is an equilateral triangle whose angles measure 60°. $\angle AOB + \angle BOC = 180°$, so $\angle BOC$ measures 120°, making the arc degree also 120°. Choice (F) gives the measure of arc AB rather than BC. Choices (G) and (J) use an incorrect triangle.

49. **A** A system of equations has no solutions if the equations have the same slope and different y-intercepts. Two linear equations have the same slope if they have the same ratio of coefficients for x and y. Set up a proportion of the coefficients: $\dfrac{12}{8} = \dfrac{3}{b}$. $12b = 24$ so $b = 2$. Choices (B), (C), (D), and (E) do not give slopes equal to that of the first equation.

50. **F** The shading above the horizontal line segment means that the y-values, which represent the number of pies Rebecca and Scott make, are never less than 1. In other words, they always make at least 1 pie, which is choice (F).

51. **B** The best way to approach this question, since it asks about the *maximum*, is check the endpoints or extremes of the graph: (7,1) and (0,4). Using the provided expression for weekly profit, $12(7) + 25(1) = \$109$, which is choice (B). Alternatively, if you started with (0,4), $12(0) + 25(4) = \$100$, choice (A). This doesn't tell you much, but moving from there on to testing (7,1) will catch you up pretty quickly. After that, if you picked choice (E), be careful! You may have reversed d and p: $12(1) + 25(7) = \$87$.

52. **K** If Rebecca and Scott made 5 pies at 3 hours each and 3 dozen cookies at 1 hour each, then they spent 18 hours baking that week. They donated $2 for every hour they spent baking, so they donated $36. The question asks what percent of that week's profit they donated, so calculate that week's profit. According to the provided expression for weekly profit, $12(3) + 25(5) = \$161$. The $36 donated, out of $161 earned, is approximately 22%, which is choice (K).

53. **A** Following the formula provided, $(w)(10) - (w)(w) = 25$. Rearranging, $10w - w^2 = 25$ becomes $w^2 - 10w + 25 = 0$. Factoring the quadratic into $(w - 5)(w - 5) = 0$, the only possible value for w is 5, choice (A).

54. **K** This formula may look complicated, but be careful with the pieces and this will be basic golden-rule algebra. If $x = B(1 + .2g)^n$, then divide both sides by $(1 + .2g)^n$ to get $\dfrac{x}{\left(1 + .2g\right)^n} = B$, which is choice (K). If you find the algebra daunting, you can also plug in simple numbers and find a target value for B.

55. **C** The main things you know for sure about m and n are that m is negative and n is positive. The least complicated option is to plug in values for m and n that adhere to the rules you're given, making m negative and n positive. Testing each answer choice using those values allows you to eliminate any that don't work out to be true. Even if you have several answer choices remaining after crossing out the ones that don't work with those numbers, picking a second set of numbers—still playing by the rules!—and testing each of your *remaining* answer choices with your new values should help you narrow it down to one. Alternatively, consider your answer choices. For choice (A), a positive number divided by a negative number will produce a negative number, not something greater than 1. Cross this answer out. For choice (B), remember that absolute value makes the inside result positive, and this will happen to both n and m. Then $|n|$ is squared, which will still be positive. A positive number, $|n|^2$, may or may not be bigger than another positive number, $|m|$, so cross this answer out. In choice (C), subtract 2 from both sides and then multiply both sides by seven, so the expression becomes simply $n > m$, which you know to be true. Keep this answer. In choice (D), squaring both m and n make both values positive, without any sense of how large or small these newly positive numbers are. Thus, even after adding 1, there's still no way to say for sure which side is larger or smaller. As for choice (E), n^{-2} and m^{-2}, which are $\dfrac{1}{n^2}$ and $\dfrac{1}{m^2}$, are both positive numbers, but again you're given no sense of which is larger or smaller. The only answer that *must* be true is choice (C).

56. J

There are several ways to think about this question. There's not a lot of information to go on, so it becomes really important to pay very careful attention to what you do know and, since you're being asked to compare two things, any relationships you can discern. Noticing that the 50° angle and the 130° angle were supplementary might lead you to match up the *a*-sides to make the big triangle pictured above on the left. If Area = $\frac{1}{2}bh$, then for $\triangle TVW$, $\frac{1}{2}bh = 45$, so $bh = 90$. Looking at $\triangle TZW$, Area = $\frac{1}{2}(2b)(h) = bh = 90$. If the area of $\triangle TZW$ is 90, and the area of $\triangle TVW$ is 45, then $90 - 45 = 45$, so the area of $\triangle XYZ$ is also 45, choice (J). Alternatively, consider the two triangles side by side, as pictured above on the right. Given that *a* and *b* are the legs of both triangles, to go from the 50° angle to the 130° angle requires dropping the height and lengthening the base proportionally. Because the base and height are inversely related this way, the area will stay constant even as the height and base shift.

57. E
The first decision you have to make is which one (or both) of these laws is useful to you. You're trying to solve for a side where you have the opposite angle, but you don't have angles to match up with either of the other two sides you know. The sides are not equivalent, so you can't assume that the angles are equivalent. Consequently, you may not have enough information to use the law of sines. The law of cosines, on the other hand, would let you solve for the missing side, *c*, knowing only the other sides and the opposite angle. Line up each piece of the formula to find that $LJ^2 = 9^2 + 6^2 - 2(9)(6)\cos 50$. Before you start calculating this value, glance at your answer choices—they aren't asking you to solve completely, just to match up the filled-in formula. Take the square root of both sides to find $LJ = \sqrt{9^2 + 6^2 - 2(9)(6)\cos 50}$, or choice (E).

58. G Break this problem up into little pieces. An arithmetic sequence has a common difference between terms, so the same number is being added to get from one term to the next. If the 7th term is 13.5 and the 11th term is 18.3, the 9th term must be exactly halfway between them at 15.9. Halfway between the 7th term and the 9th term is the 8th term, which would be at 14.7. If the 7th term is 13.5 and the 8th term is 14.7, then the common difference between terms is 1.2. Working backward from the 7th term, the 6th term is 12.3, the 5th term is 11.1, the 4th term is 9.9, the 3rd term is 8.7, the 2nd term is 7.5, and the 1st term is 6.3. Adding up the first three terms, $6.3 + 7.5 + 8.7 = 22.5$, which is choice (G). There is a formula for arithmetic sequences, but when you're dealing with relatively small numbers in relatively small quantities, often the most reliable thing to do is simply write it out.

59. C If the *only* possible value for w is 8, then the quadratic in factored form is $(w - 8)(w - 8) = 0$. Expanding this by FOILing gives you $w^2 - 16w + 64 = 0$. Line this up with the original equation to find that p must be 16, and q must be 64. With your answer choices, make sure you know what you're looking for—if you picked choice (E), you may have solved for q instead of p.

60. F The simplest thing to do is to start by determining which values the problem is describing. Since it wants the numbers that are 4 units from –1, only two points satisfy that: –5 and 3. If you're having trouble thinking about that, simply draw a number line and count it out.

If the answer choices describe the solution set of –5 and 3, then you can test these values in each of the answer choices to eliminate ones that don't work. In choice (F), $|3 + 1| = 4$ and $|-5 + 1| = 4$. Both values work, so this will be your answer. In choice (G), $|3 - 1| \neq 4$, so eliminate that. In choice (H), $|3 + 4| \neq 1$, so eliminate that. In choice (J), $|-5 - 4| \neq 1$, so eliminate that, too. In choice (K), $|3 + 4| \neq 1$, so eliminate that.

NOTES

NOTES

NOTES

NOTES

NOTES

NOTES